MUSIC TOGETHER®

TAMBOURINE

Developed by the Center for Music and Young Children®

Kenneth K. Guilmartin
Founder/Director
Center for Music and Young Children
Princeton, New Jersey

Lili M. Levinowitz, Ph.D.
Professor of Music Education
Rowan University
Glassboro, New Jersey

AUTHORS

Kenneth K. Guilmartin conceived and led the development of the innovative Music Together program for the Center for Music and Young Children, which he founded in 1985. He has composed numerous scores for off-Broadway and regional theatre productions and is a popular presenter at early childhood and music educator conferences. He has created music programs and conducted teacher trainings for early childhood centers nationwide. A graduate of Swarthmore College, he studied composition and pedagogy at Manhattan School of Music and is certified in Dalcroze Eurhythmics by the Manhattan Dalcroze Institute.

Lili M. Levinowitz, Ph.D., is Professor of Music Education at Rowan University. She is a national authority on early childhood music and is actively involved in teaching very young children as well as graduate students. Her articles appear frequently in professional journals and popular magazines. She received her Ph.D. from Temple University where she was director of the Children's Music Development Program.

The authors gratefully acknowledge Lyn Ransom, D.M.A., Director of Program Development at the Center for Music and Young Children, for her contributions to this book as a curriculum consultant and writer.

The Center for Music and Young Children® (CMYC), developer of Music Together, was founded in 1985. CMYC is committed to helping families, caregivers, and early childhood professionals rediscover the pleasure and educational value of informal musical experiences. Rather than emphasizing traditional music performances, CMYC encourages family participation in spontaneous musical activity occurring within the context of daily life. CMYC recognizes that all children are musical and that every child needs a stimulating, supportive music environment to achieve basic competence in the wonderful human capacity for music-making.

Music Together is a music and movement approach to early childhood music development for infant, toddler, preschool, and kindergarten children and their parents, teachers, and other primary caregivers. Originally offered to the public in 1987, it pioneered the concept of a research-based, developmentally appropriate early childhood music curriculum that strongly emphasizes and facilitates adult involvement.

The Music Together approach develops every child's birthright of basic music competence by encouraging the actual experiencing of music rather than the learning of concepts or information about music. Music Together began as an educational project of the Center for Music and Young Children and is now enjoyed by thousands of families in the United States and abroad.

For further information about Music Together programs, teacher training, parent education, child-friendly instruments, or classes, both national and international, please contact:

Music Together LLC
66 Witherspoon Street, Princeton NJ 08542
(800) 728-2692
www.musictogether.com

Music Together: "Tambourine" Song Collection

©2010 Music Together LLC. No part of this publication may be photocopied, recorded, stored, transmitted, or reproduced in any form or by any means, electronic, mechanical, or otherwise, without prior written permission of Music Together, 66 Witherspoon Street, Princeton NJ 08542 (800) 728-2692.

Please note that the arrangements and adaptations of traditional material in this collection have been created by the authors and are protected by copyright.

Every reasonable effort has been made to identify and locate copyright holders of the material in this songbook. Any omission is inadvertent and will be corrected by contacting Music Together.

Music Together, Center for Music and Young Children, and CMYC are registered trademarks. Music Together logo art ©1992–2002 Music Together LLC. Music Together logo designs and song illustrations are by Main Street Design, Pennington NJ.

Read more about FSC Certification on the inside back cover.

CONTENTS

Making the Most of Your Class Experience 5
You and Your Child Can Learn Music! 6
How to Use this Book 10
How to Reach Us 10
Our Family of Song Collections 11
Imagine 12
Betty Martin 19
Cradle Song..29
Ding Dong, Ding Dong 41
Goodbye, So Long, Farewell..47
Good News 45
Green and Blue 22
Hello Song 13
Hey Ya Na...23
Hippity, Happity, Hoppity 36
Merry-Go-Round..39
Old Brass Wagon 15
One Little Owl 21
Pawpaw Patch 37
Raisins and Almonds...46
Ride-O 16
Round Robin 17
Scarborough Fair 43
Secrets 40
See the Pony Galloping 24
Sneakin' 'Round the Room 35
Tambourine Jam 30
This 'n' That 42
Tingalayo..18
Tricks with Sticks...26
Wedding Dance 25
Musical Memories..48
Glossary 50
Guitar Reference Chart...51
References/Acknowledgments 52

MAKING THE MOST OF YOUR CLASS EXPERIENCE

Reading this preface will help you maximize your class experience. We will discuss the basic Music Together philosophy, how children learn, what parents can do in class, how to use the recording and songbook (even if you don't read music), and how to start making music at home.

Not every parent feels comfortable in class at first. You may have had a difficult time with music or music lessons as a child, or you may have grown up with no music in your life. In spite of your own past experiences, you have taken a major musical step for your child by enrolling in this class. We invite you to be childlike again and to experience music as if it were new to you. Forget your images of perfect performances and music for the talented few—we'll help you find ways to enjoy music so your child will catch your spirit and enjoy it, too.

Brothers and sisters can attend class together. One of the goals of Music Together is to bring music back to family life. Can you imagine sitting around as a family and singing instead of watching TV or playing computer games? As technology increases, the importance of non-technical group interaction also increases, especially at home. We think that family music-making can be a wonderful activity shared by brothers, sisters, parents, relatives, and even nannies. For this reason, siblings are encouraged to attend class together, so that they will experience the same music and movement activities and will want to recreate them at home together.

Classes with children of many ages are educationally sound. The younger children learn by observing and imitating the older ones; the older children benefit from singing to, moving with, and being appreciated by the younger ones. Most importantly, vocal discoveries, movement ideas, or ways to play an instrument are communicated freely from child to child, regardless of age or stage of development. Leading child psychologists endorse mixed-age groupings because children learn more easily and more deeply there than in single-age classes.

It is never too early or too late to begin Music Together classes. In class you will experience music that is fun, accessible, and sophisticated, so that people of many ages can enjoy it. Because adults and children enter the experience at many different levels, each person comes away with what he needs for his own musical growth. It is like a musical buffet: each person picks his or her favorite foods today, but may choose something different tomorrow, depending upon tastes and the nourishment needed. A toddler, an infant, or a four-year-old may take different things home from a Music Together class, but each will find many things that meet his or her needs on any given day. In this way, a child may begin classes at any age and will continue to grow musically throughout succeeding semesters.

When possible, we encourage parents to enroll children in Music Together as newborns. Babies are especially receptive to sounds, perhaps even more than to what they see. Infancy is an excellent time for a child to learn music, because infants expand their tonal vocabulary rapidly. Because they learn so fast, we encourage parents to bring babies to mixed-age classes with their older siblings or to enroll in a Music Together Babies Class (for eight-month-olds or younger). If you or your friends have an infant, please consider enrolling in this class if it is offered in your area.

A CHILD'S WISH LIST

I wish you would sing to me all day long. I want you to put your face close to mine and look into my eyes and sing with a mouth that's big and expressive. I hope you will also hold me and dance and tap lightly on my arms and legs. I want this sweet rhythmic movement several times a day. I'm an infant.

I want you to sing and play musically while you change my diaper, while we ride in the car, while you dance with me, when we go for a walk, when we take a bath. I love the stuff of music—the red drum, the sound from the speakers, the songs with silly sneezes and funny movements. I love to dance up and down when I hear music! I love being swung to slow music or bounced to fast music or danced with in a circle. I'm a toddler.

I wish I could do it myself, and I can. I can remember the words to songs—the tune, too. I can enter my own world and sing to myself for hours or play in my own one-person band. I like the way I make music, I like to watch others make music, and I'd like to do some of the things the music teacher does. I really love it when my family will dance and play instruments with me. I'm a three-year-old.

Music is one of my specialties. I love learning exactly how to do a clapping pattern or a dance step. I like to play instruments the real way. I love to practice the things I'm interested in, and I know when I get things "right" according to me. I'm attracted to other kids who can do great things in music, and I'm beginning to feel like I need music every day and maybe for the rest of my life. I'm four-and-a-half, and proud of it!

YOU AND YOUR CHILD CAN LEARN MUSIC!

How do people learn music? How do infants learn? Toddlers? Four-year-olds? Early childhood experts believe that each child learns from rich and varied music experiences and that, given a variety of engaging activities, each child will learn the things she is ready to learn at any given moment. This approach, which is often called "developmentally appropriate practice," allows each child to be responsible for his own learning and helps adults view children's growth through stages of development, not ages.

Children learn through play. Your child may want to listen, move, sing, or play an instrument at home, sometimes for extended periods of time. The child is recalling, recounting, experimenting, practicing, and creating through play. Sometimes he will want to play alone, and sometimes, more than anything else, he will want you to join him. Take your cues from your child and see what happens!

Here are the four basic ideas of the Music Together philosophy. You can read more about these ideas in the parent guide, and you may discuss them briefly in class and at parent education evenings.

- All children are musical.
- All children can achieve basic music competence.
- The participation and modeling of parents and caregivers is essential to a child's music growth.
- Young children's musical growth occurs best in a playful, musically rich, and developmentally appropriate setting, free of direct instruction and performance pressure, where learning activities are accessible, interesting, and fun for both children and adults.

All children are musical.

You may be reassured to know that all children are musical and that all adults are, too! You don't need to wonder if your child has musical talent: all children do. You needn't wonder if you have any musical talent: you do! It may be resting there, undiscovered and unused, but it's there. Music Together classes can help you develop your talent, as well as your child's.

In Western culture, we tend to believe that musical talent or aptitude is given to only a few. We tend to believe that these "talented" people are the ones who grow up to be rock stars, symphony orchestra players, or concert pianists. In actual fact, music aptitude or talent is normally distributed in a "bell curve" manner, that is, music aptitude is distributed throughout the population just as talent in language, math, visual art, architecture, computer engineering, dance, and other areas are. In fact, eighty-four percent of the population is born with enough music aptitude to play in a symphony orchestra, and only two percent of the population is born with either exceptionally high or low music intelligence.

So, despite your fears that either you or your child may not have any musical talent, rest assured that all of you have some level of music aptitude. You will be in a class where your aptitude will be exercised and your child's will be nurtured.

To learn more about this, you can read Edwin Gordon's work on music aptitude or Howard Gardner's theories of multiple intelligences. These are referenced in the back of this book, along with other publications of interest.

All children can achieve basic music competence.

Music Together defines basic music competence in very simple terms. A child is musically competent when he or she can sing in tune with accurate rhythm.

This sounds basic—everyone should be able to carry a tune, right? Do an experiment: think of six friends and write down their names. Now check off the ones that you know who can carry a tune by themselves, without a radio, CD, or keyboard. You may find that one or none out of six can sing. In the general population in the US, fewer and fewer people can carry a tune or keep a beat now, even though they once had the potential to do so. This is unfortunate since all children have musical talent or aptitude and all children can achieve this skill.

If your child experiences interesting music in class and experiments with that music at home for several years during early childhood, he or she is more likely to achieve basic music competence by the age of three or four. This is an astounding statement, although it sounds simple. By age three or four, children who have had enough early music experience can usually sing in tune with accurate rhythm. This means that these children can sing and keep a beat as well or better than much of the adult population! Given early exposure to good musical models, it is completely normal for young children to sing, create songs, move rhythmically, play instruments in a steady tempo, feel at home with unusual meters, improvise rhythmically, and enjoy music-making.

If your child has active experience with a wealth of interesting songs and rhythmic movement before the age of five, he or she is likely to have an excellent music and movement vocabulary for the rest of his or her life. If a child has less experience in music, and therefore less opportunity to experiment with it, he may reach basic music competence at age five or six, but it could be as late as third grade, or never. Some children never achieve basic music competence because they have had inadequate experience in music. This is becoming more and more common as music-making becomes less important in our culture and family life. The richness, variety, and amount of your child's early experience in music affects both what he achieves and the delight he derives.

Tonal competence. You can watch your child develop and notice when she can sing an entire song with the correct melody. When a child can sing the melody beginning on different notes, that is, when the child can maintain the melodic patterns even though the key is changed, we know that the child is competent in melody. She can hear the melody in her mind and can think flexibly about the tonal patterns of the tune. She can remember and recall a tune in order to play it or to make up new words to it. This inner hearing ability is key to making music, both alone and in groups, and will help your child considerably if she begins to study an instrument.

Rhythm competence. You can also notice your child developing rhythmically. When he can say a rhythmic chant correctly at different tempos or speeds, then we know he can maintain the rhythmic patterns through his thought process, not just by rote memorization. This shows that he is competent in rhythm. When a child is competent in both rhythm and melody, we say he has achieved basic music competence. While musical competence may be difficult for many adults to achieve, it is *normal* for children who have had early childhood music experiences. You are to be congratulated for providing music-making experiences for your child when he is most ready to learn.

Usually a child becomes competent in one area several months or even years earlier than in the other. Researchers have noted that most people have an affinity for either pitch or rhythm and may achieve competence in one area sooner than the other. Children who love to move and who respond to music by dancing rather than singing may be more attracted to the rhythmic aspects of music. Young children who respond to music more by singing along, listening intently, or playing an instrument may be more melodic or tonal in nature.

Do you think your child is more attracted to rhythm or pitch? You may want to write down what you notice on the page entitled "Musical Memories." When he is older, he will be very interested in your memories of his musical experiences as a child.

While many children and adults may have a stronger affinity for either melody or rhythm, some have an equal attraction to both. It's like walking and talking. Some children start to do both at once; others develop one skill sooner than the other. Both are interesting for parents to notice, but neither predicts how well a child will walk, talk, or make music as an adult.

The participation and modeling of parents and caregivers is essential to a child's musical growth.

You may not believe this, but it is true. The parent or primary caregiver is the child's most important music teacher! It is the parent or caregiver alone that can teach a young child to enjoy music-making. A music teacher can help your child learn skills and content, but only you can help your child enjoy music. The reason for this is simple. Young children naturally want to be like their parents and enjoy the same things they do—if the parents swim, the children will; if the parents read, the children will; if the parents make music, the children will, too.

You may not want the responsibility of being your child's most important musical influence, but remember, the Music Together teacher leads the songs, provides opportunities to learn skills, and helps you figure out what to do. All you have to do is enjoy music and movement and communicate that in simple, direct ways to your child. Then, because music is such a strong form of communication, you will not need to tell your child, "I just love making music. Look at how much fun it is for me to play a shaker and sing!" Your child will sense that from feeling your body move and hearing you sing in whatever voice you have. Music can be one of the most wonderful nonverbal means of communication that you will experience together.

In this songbook, you will read about a child's wish list for music class and the parent's path for helping them. Enjoy these lists, then think about your child. Perhaps you would like to rewrite the music wish list from your own child's point of view. What do you think she would like you to do?

Young children's musical growth occurs best in a playful, musically rich, and developmentally appropriate setting.

This setting for your child is free of direct instruction and performance pressure. Learning activities are accessible, interesting and fun for both children and adults. In class, you will notice that there is a good deal of childlike play. This is because children learn through play and experimentation. In class you will experience music, rather than learn facts about it. You will be invited to participate in music-making, from simply keeping a beat with egg shakers to improvising rhythms in the play-along. This playful music participation is the opposite of performance pressure—there are no performance rules or expectations. You and your child will be encouraged to enter into activities at your own comfort level and participate freely.

Your child may sometimes want to absorb the activity without participating: this is expected. You may want to participate quietly at first, and this is also fine. The actual activities are designed to be interesting to adults and children alike, and they provide for many levels of participation.

THE PARENT'S PATH

In class, join in the singing without judging your participation. Even if you feel shy or hesitant or musically inexperienced, find a way to relax and enjoy singing the songs. Your child will know if you genuinely enjoy making music, so find a way that works authentically for you.

Join in the moving and dancing activities in class, and share that enjoyment physically with your child. He will understand that moving is fun and a good thing to do when he sees you swaying, clapping, stomping, rocking, and jumping.

Take cues from your child and respond musically. If your child "coos" on a pitch, return the sound. If your child sings on the way to the grocery store, sing with her. If your child asks for the Music Together recording and brings an instrument to you, try to stop what you are doing and play with your child.

Respond to your child in nonverbal ways. That is, respond musically without talking, so your child will grow in his music experience and will understand that you enjoy music communication and play. Look at him when you sing together, join in his beat on the drum, or imitate his "dance." You might even smile at your child when you do something really silly to let him know that you're just playing and having fun.

As your familiarity with the program grows, you may want to refer back to the four concepts just discussed: All children are musical. All children can achieve basic music competence. The participation and modeling of parents and caregivers is essential to a child's musical growth. Young children's musical growth occurs best in a playful, musically rich, and developmentally appropriate setting, free of direct instruction and performance pressure, where learning activities are accessible, interesting, and fun for both children and adults.

We invite you to share any music, dance, or movement skills you have with the class. In most families, the child is happy that the parent can contribute something special to class activities. If you have an instrument, bring it, especially for the play-along. If you have a beautiful voice and can hear harmonies, sing out freely. If you have a background in dance, improvise at your own level in class, and others will learn from you.

Move to music, play instruments, and sing at home often. You are the real teacher for your child's enjoyment of music, so plan to make music together several times during the week. Some families make music after breakfast every Saturday morning. Others sing and play instruments just after supper. Others keep a basket of instruments and the songbook in the car for making music on trips. Use the songbook and recording to stimulate family music-making. Play and experiment together often and see what happens.

SPECIAL SETTINGS

Nannies. Many families send their primary daytime caregiver to class with their child. Some nannies are very comfortable with music-making and use the Music Together activities to enliven the child's time at home. Other nannies are less comfortable with music-making, and may need some direction from you. Try to imagine the questions she could ask. What is expected of me in a music class? Do I have to be responsible for anything in particular at the class? At home? How am I supposed to use the songbook? The recording? You may want to give the nanny specific assignments, for example, to play with music and your child every day for at least a half-hour. Invite her to read the introduction to this book, and ask her to report back to you on the child's actions during class. It may take a few months to help the nanny feel comfortable singing, dancing, creating, observing, and playing in class and at home, but what a wonderful and valuable use of the time she and your child spend together. When there is a parent education evening or class you can attend, try to attend with the nanny so she can model her participation after yours.

Babysitters. These occasional caregivers are important to family life and may appreciate guidance. If you keep a book of notes and activity suggestions for babysitters, be sure to write about the Music Together CD, songbook, and activities. You might suggest that the babysitter try at least three or four music activities each time he or she stays with your child. The simple instructions written under each song will be a good guide. When you return home, ask the babysitter about the music activities and how your child or children responded.

Older children. In school and out of school, parents and teachers report that these songs are among the favorites of children through third grade and higher.

Older citizens. Because the songs in this collection are accessible but sophisticated, they appeal to people of many ages. Grandparents and caregivers may find a new joy in life when they discover how much fun it is to sing and dance with their little ones! However, grandparents may tend to instruct children as they were instructed in grade school. You may need to explain current thinking in music development in order for them to relax, play, and have fun with music.

Individuals with special needs. Parents and teachers involved with Music Together recount story after story about the value of this music for inspiring joy and language. People with Alzheimer's disease often enjoy music, and the Music Together songs are often favorites. Many times people who have lost the ability to speak can nevertheless sing the texts to songs. In addition, children with special needs often find the activities engaging. Music Together recordings won't provide a cure, but they can provide hours of happiness, music-making, and family comfort for people of all ages.

Preschool and childcare. In many communities, Music Together is a vital part of preschool programs, and children participate in regular music classes as part of their daily routine. Parents receive materials to take home, so that they can make music with their children, whether or not they are able to visit the daytime classes. In addition, the Music Together specialist, along with the supporting materials, help teachers and aides to understand and facilitate the process of music development. Current research continues to confirm that music activities can play a powerful role in a child's development. When it is time for you to choose a preschool or childcare center, be sure to ask about its music program.

Family reunions. Many families get together regularly with aunts, uncles, grandparents, new babies, and lots of cousins. Why not bring a Music Together CD or songbook and lead some family activities? Let your children choose the songs or dances they especially enjoy, and encourage teenagers or older children to help the little ones. If you join in, leading gently when necessary, other children and parents will feel comfortable participating. You might begin the sing-along with songs you think the extended family might know; then move to less familiar songs. If you take a basket of instruments and end with a play-along, you'll be making many children happy. Encourage the grandparents, especially, to join the music-making. They generally love to watch children and are often very spontaneous in the way they make music. A child may want to be the Music Together teacher and direct the class. Won't it be fun to be the student?

HOW TO USE THIS BOOK

This book will be a wonderful resource for you. You can use it to help you recall activities from class or to remember the words to songs. Take some time to put the recording on and follow the words as you hear the songs, so you can become familiar with the music. Glance over the activity suggestions as you listen.

If you don't read music, use the book occasionally to point out words or pictures to your child as you sing or hear them. Over time, both of you will make connections between the notes on the page and the notes you hear. You may notice that music notes sometimes appear in a child's drawings just like other symbols in a child's life, like the "ABCs." Parents who play instruments "by ear" may find that using the book to follow or remember the music will help them play better and understand more.

If you do read music, you will enjoy playing or singing through the collection. Parents who used to play when they were younger may delight in taking a forgotten instrument out of the case and playing through the songs. Your child will notice that you read the music and play your instrument and might be interested in doing the same thing. Parents and caregivers who do read music will be able to play along either with or in place of the recording.

Try out the family activities you can do at home. Each music page contains several ideas for interacting with your child. Many of these ideas will be familiar to you from class, but some will be new and especially fun to try at home. Some activity suggestions are for a particular age group, others are for a setting, others are designed to inspire movement or instrument play. Experiment with these suggestions. Jot down what your child liked and write in other ideas you think of, so your songbook becomes a recipe book for a good family time.

Listen for featured instruments on the recording. In the colored sidebar, there are drawings of instruments featured on the recording. When you look at the book with an older child, point out the instruments as you hear them on the recording. If the featured instrument is one which a child could manage safely and enjoyably, try to provide it, so she can play along at home.

Play "found" and real instruments with the recording. You may want to collect some household objects that make sounds and keep them handy in a basket or drawer so they can come out easily for music-making. Play them often, both with the recording and without. Parents who play instruments will be especially at home with the play-along, in which everyone improvises at his own level, both children and adults. Portable instruments like the guitar, clarinet, or harmonica can go on family outings and help you make music anywhere, any time. To order instruments that are well constructed, nontoxic, and child-friendly, please visit our online store at www.musictogether.com.

Look at the songbook illustrations with your child. You will notice that several songs are illustrated with beautiful woodcuts. Take time to look at these with your child and let her take the lead in pointing out what she sees. Sing the song while you look at the picture, and enjoy the richness of visual art and music combined. Many songs do not have illustrations, so this makes a perfect opportunity for your child to draw or paint something. Older children may enjoy hanging their pictures or collecting them in a personal songbook.

Use the songbook as a storybook. It is especially nice to use the Music Together songbooks at bedtime or naptime. The songs and pictures may remind the child of pleasurable experiences with you, helping him to fall asleep easily. The routine quiet of nap or bed may make the child receptive to your singing the lullabies or songs, so put aside your own opinion of your voice for a moment, and sing to your young child with the sweetest voice she knows!

HOW TO REACH US

Your Music Together center director or teacher has been trained in children's music learning from birth to age five. Take time to think about music development questions you would like to discuss, and ask your teacher before or after class.

You may also contact the Center for Music and Young Children directly. To find out about classes for friends or relatives in other states or to discuss doing special projects with us, please call or visit our website. We are especially interested in knowing how Music Together classes help your children enjoy and learn music, both now and as they mature. We also value knowing how the program helps or inspires your family to make music, so do write and tell us! We would enjoy hearing from you.

Center for Music and Young Children
66 Witherspoon Street, Princeton NJ 08542
(800) 728-2692 • www.musictogether.com

STICKS **DRUM** **FIDDLE** **TRIANGLE**

SONG COLLECTIONS

The Center for Music and Young Children has developed nine non-sequential song collections, each characterized by its own graphic, color, and instrument. These collections each include a recording and songbook and are designed to be used one collection per semester. The collections are not sequential. A family can begin Music Together classes at any semester with any collection.

This semester you will take part in the rich and balanced music experiences of the current collection. In your next Music Together semester, you will receive a new songbook and recording. You will learn new songs, dances, and movement activities. You will learn more about your child's musical growth and enjoyment. Your child will thrive on the continuity from class to class, and if you attend for three consecutive years, you will experience all nine song collections—what a wealth of music for your family to enjoy!

TAMBOURINE

The music is pitched in just the right range for children's voices and includes songs, rhythmic chants, tonal and rhythm patterns, and instrumental play-alongs, all in a rich variety of tonalities and meters. Original songs and arrangements by the program coauthors make these collections unique. Outstanding instrumentalists play a variety of instruments, such as guitar, bass, flutes, keyboards, and percussion. And all of the songs are suitable for mixed-age groups, perfect for childcare centers or families with children of different ages.

Music Together's song collections are research-based and artistically conceived and produced. They are also classroom- and family-tested. Since 1987, the feedback of hundreds of teachers and thousands of families has been incorporated into these constantly evolving materials.

MARACAS **BONGOS** **BELLS** **FLUTE**

Imagine what your child experiences in a Music Together class! There are wonderful sounds, interesting movements, instruments to play, other children to watch, silly things to laugh at, an inviting teacher to follow, and music that your child loves! Your child is in class with you or the caregiver you select, and this grownup holds him, hugs him, sings, and loves making music, too! What a comfortable and exciting experience!

Going to Music Together can be wonderful for a parent, too. You may love the activities and love seeing your child's response. It is exceptionally satisfying for a parent to have found a program that allows his or her child to flourish! You will learn about music development in class, through special attention given to individual children. You will meet other adults and may even become a favorite grownup for another child. You will learn songs, movement activities, and dances which are fun in themselves and provide for family music-making at home.

One of the delights of becoming involved in Music Together is discovering or rediscovering your own relationship to music. You may discover that you love to sing, or you may find that the classes provide just the opportunity you need to get out an instrument you haven't played for years. Drumming or dancing may feel new and wonderful, especially removed from the anxieties of high school or college performance experiences. This musical awakening has happened for hundreds of parents who have found—or rediscovered—the great satisfaction and joy in making music with their children. Welcome!

Hello Song

K. Guilmartin

This catchy tune is a favorite, because children love musical play with names.

Hel - lo____ ev - 'ry - bo - dy,____ so glad to see you!

Hel - lo____ ev - 'ry - bo - dy,____ I'm so glad to see you!

Hel - lo____ to (name),____ so glad to see you!

Hel - lo____ to (different name), so glad to see you, too!

Sing the "Hello Song" using your child's name or the names of friends, relatives, pets, or dolls. As you sing, sway gently back and forth to the beat, so your child sees and feels the pulse. Sing this cheerful song as a ritual when you first see your child in the morning or any time you greet him.

Variations: Try using it as a peek-a-boo song, singing a phrase at a time as you pop out from behind a scarf, newspaper, or other object. Honor special visitors by singing them the "Hello Song," and incorporate it into special parties or family meals.

Older children will enjoy a "silly" version. For example, sing to various unlikely objects, such as the clock, the spoon, or your nose: "Hello, to my sneaker, so glad to see you!" Then you can get them to sing "hello" to other objects, by pointing to them during the song. Another good "silly" game is to sing the wrong names of family or friends. Make a mistake, then ask the children to show you how to do it right. Preschoolers love this!

Infants/toddlers: Babies are very focused on faces, especially mouths. So sing close to your baby, so he can feel your energy, sense the rhythm and your breathing, and see your facial expression. Hug your child and sway with her on your lap. Every time you greet each other after being apart, give your child some lap time and a few repetitions of this song. Rituals like this mean a lot to young children. They also help children grow musically, because musical expression becomes a natural part of daily life.

Recording: Guitar, bass, shaker, tambourine

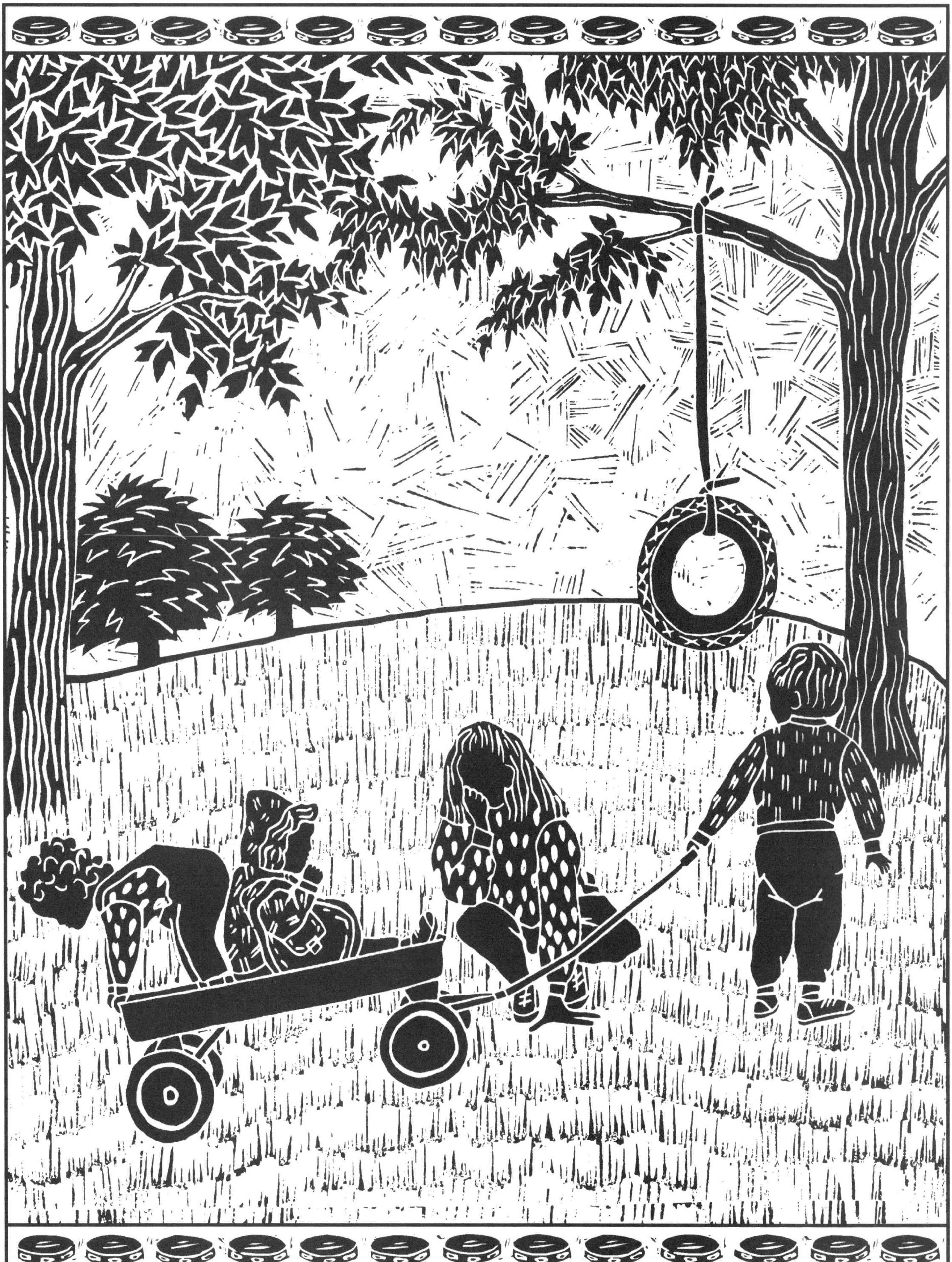

Hello Song

K. Guilmartin

Moderately

Hel - lo_____ ev - 'ry - bo - dy,_____ so glad to see you!

Hel - lo_____ ev - 'ry - bo - dy,_____ I'm so glad to see you!

Hel - lo_____ to (name),_____ so glad to see you!

Hel - lo_____ to (different name), so glad to see you, too!

This catchy tune is a favorite, because children love musical play with names.

Sing the "Hello Song" using your child's name or the names of friends, relatives, pets, or dolls. As you sing, sway gently back and forth to the beat, so your child sees and feels the pulse. Sing this cheerful song as a ritual when you first see your child in the morning or any time you greet him.

Variations: Try using it as a peek-a-boo song, singing a phrase at a time as you pop out from behind a scarf, newspaper, or other object. Honor special visitors by singing them the "Hello Song," and incorporate it into special parties or family meals.

Older children will enjoy a "silly" version. For example, sing to various unlikely objects, such as the clock, the spoon, or your nose: "Hello, to my sneaker, so glad to see you!" Then you can get them to sing "hello" to other objects, by pointing to them during the song. Another good "silly" game is to sing the wrong names of family or friends. Make a mistake, then ask the children to show you how to do it right. Preschoolers love this!

Infants/toddlers: Babies are very focused on faces, especially mouths. So sing close to your baby, so he can feel your energy, sense the rhythm and your breathing, and see your facial expression. Hug your child and sway with her on your lap. Every time you greet each other after being apart, give your child some lap time and a few repetitions of this song. Rituals like this mean a lot to young children. They also help children grow musically, because musical expression becomes a natural part of daily life.

Recording: Guitar, bass, shaker, tambourine

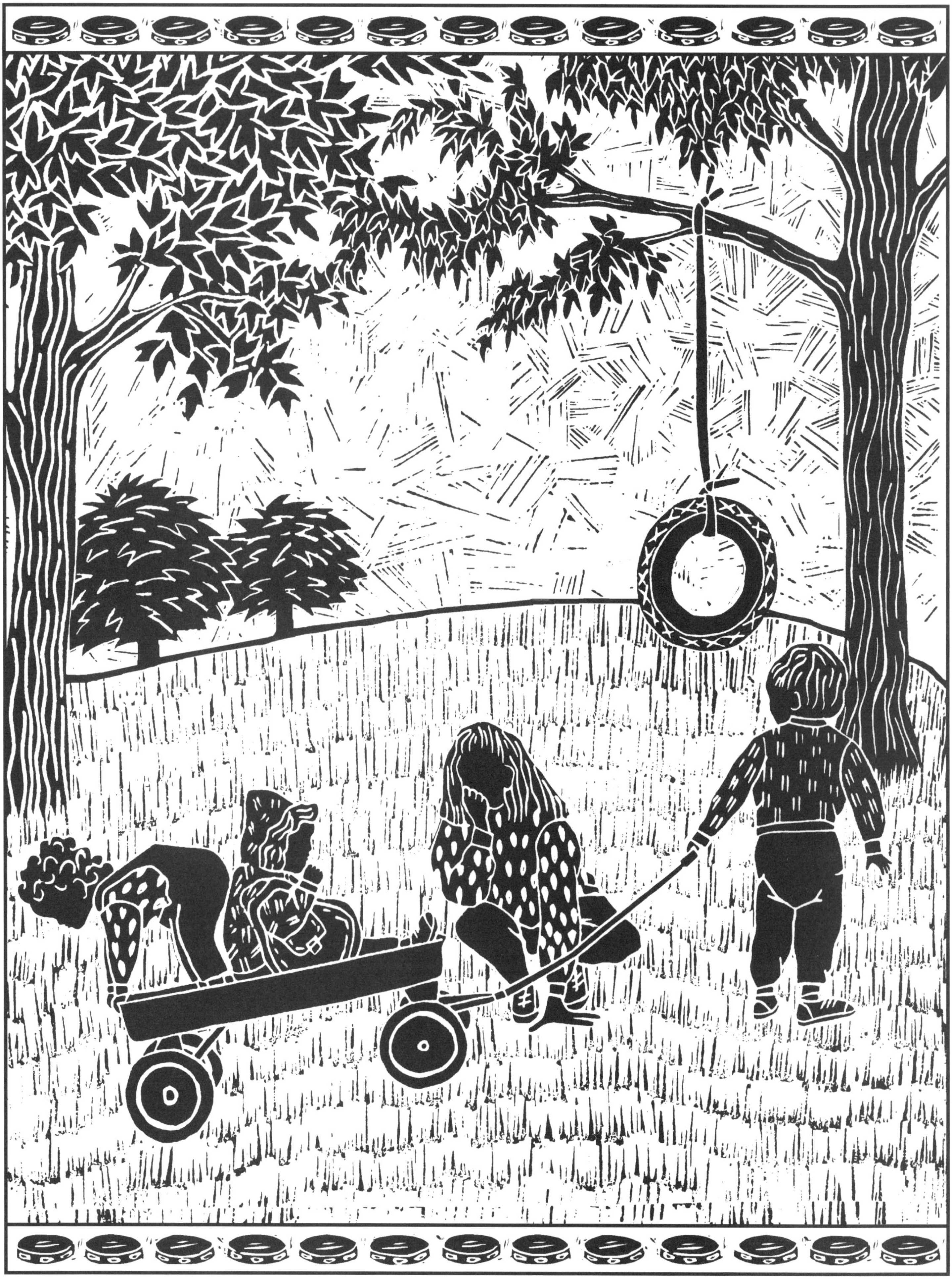

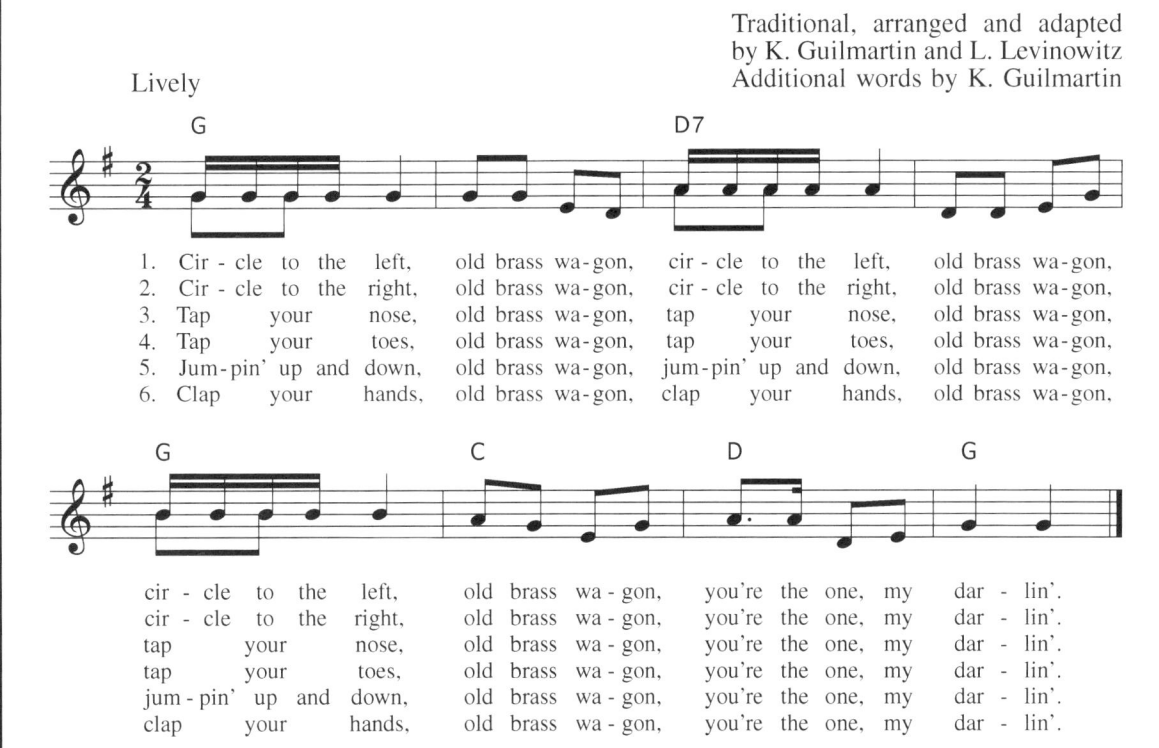

Old Brass Wagon

*Traditional, arranged and adapted
by K. Guilmartin and L. Levinowitz
Additional words by K. Guilmartin*

Lively

1. Cir - cle to the left, old brass wa-gon, cir - cle to the left, old brass wa-gon,
2. Cir - cle to the right, old brass wa-gon, cir - cle to the right, old brass wa-gon,
3. Tap your nose, old brass wa-gon, tap your nose, old brass wa-gon,
4. Tap your toes, old brass wa-gon, tap your toes, old brass wa-gon,
5. Jum-pin' up and down, old brass wa-gon, jum-pin' up and down, old brass wa-gon,
6. Clap your hands, old brass wa-gon, clap your hands, old brass wa-gon,

cir - cle to the left, old brass wa - gon, you're the one, my dar - lin'.
cir - cle to the right, old brass wa - gon, you're the one, my dar - lin'.
tap your nose, old brass wa - gon, you're the one, my dar - lin'.
tap your toes, old brass wa - gon, you're the one, my dar - lin'.
jum - pin' up and down, old brass wa - gon, you're the one, my dar - lin'.
clap your hands, old brass wa - gon, you're the one, my dar - lin'.

You're the one, my darlin'.

Put on the CD and get everyone in your family up on their feet! Sing along as you do the movements suggested on the recording—"circle to the left," "circle to the right," and so on. In the instrumental break, repeat these movements or improvise some of your own (see "large movement" below). When your family knows the song, sing and dance without the recording.

Lap song: Sing when your family is sitting around relaxing. Bounce babies and toddlers on your lap while you sing "bouncin' up and down." Play patty-cake with older children. Hug your child on the words "you're the one, my darlin'."

Songbook illustration: Ask you child what she sees in the picture, then sing her answer. For example, "Go for a ride, old brass wagon," or "Swing on the tire, old brass wagon." If she doesn't volunteer any observations, sing some of your own.

Large movement: Think up other ways to move: "Swing your arm, old brass wagon," or "Wiggle your hips, old brass wagon." Try anything your children or their playmates offer.

History: "Old Brass Wagon" is an old square dance tune, popular in pioneer times.

Recording: Piano, guitar, bass, violin, tambourine, tone block, cowbell

Ride-O

Traditional, arranged and
adapted with new words by
K. Guilmartin and L. Levinowitz

VERSE
Bouncy

1, 2. *(sing on "doo," "dee," or any other syllable)*
3. Dri - ving, dri - ving, dri - ving, *etc.*
4. Zoom, zoom, zoom, zoom, zoom, zoom! *etc.*
5. Ti - ckle, ti - ckle, ti - ckle, *etc.*
6. La, la, la, la, la, la, *etc.*

(To INTERLUDE after verses 2, 4 and 6)

INTERLUDE

Voices: *(sing on "la")*
Instruments:

To VERSE

Let's go for a ride!

Seat your child next to you or on your lap and say, "Let's go for a ride!" Sing on "doo," "dee," or another syllable and move rhythmically as if riding horses or driving cars, trucks, bicycles, etc.

Claps 'n' taps: Clap your hands, or tap parts of your body such as your legs, head, shoulders, nose, etc. Take turns leading this tapping play. Put young children on your lap and bounce, tap, or tickle.

Vocal play: Sing using silly or unusual sounds like "buzz," "ding," or "waah" (crying sounds). Sing in a deep, loud voice on "ho, ho, ho," and in a high, squeaky voice on "hee, hee, hee."

Infants and toddlers: Try singing this song as you go about your daily activities. For example, after a bath you can sing and move the towel rhythmically as you dry your child, using "la," "da," or one of your child's favorite sounds. Or sing about your child as he practices new physical skills: "rolling," "crawling," "waving," and "walking."

Older children: Vary the loudness and tempo to suit your child's favorite ways of moving. For example, you might do a brisk "marching" for one repetition, then a slower, quieter "sleeping" verse, followed by a loud and fast "chasing" verse. Ask them for ideas and whether they want a turn being the leader.

Recording: Guitar, bass, flute, shaker, woodblock, triangle

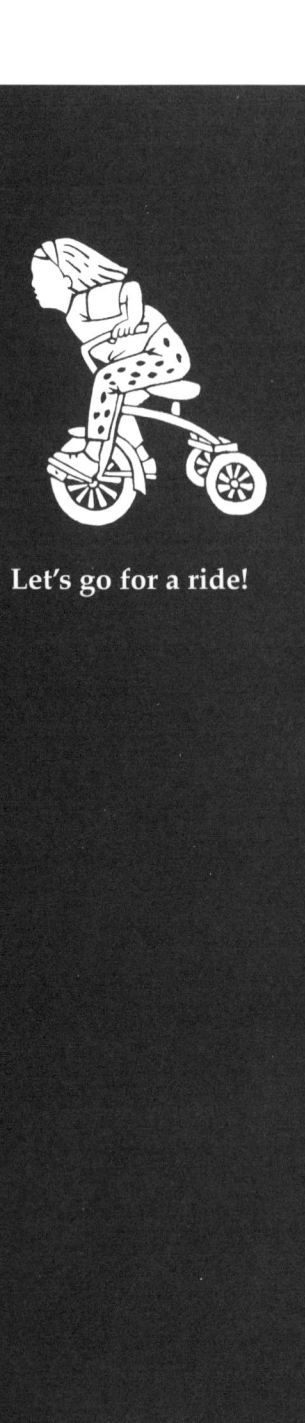

Round Robin

Rebecca Frezza

Round for 3 or more voices

Ro - bin red breast, Crow fly - ing 'round.

Nut - hatch hop - ping down the tree, Chick-a - dee - dee - dee - dee - dee!

Caw, caw, caw, caw. Chick-a-

dee - dee - dee, Chick - a - dee - dee - dee, Chick - a - dee - dee - dee, Chick - a - dee - dee - dee.

To create a round, additional voices can begin singing when the first voice reaches the asterisk (*).

Sing along with the birds.

Use your hand to create a bird, swooping it through the air or moving your thumb and fingers like a beak. Make some bird sounds, then create movements as you begin to sing:

Robin: Open and close your bird "beak" on the beat.
Crow: Make your hand flat like a wing and "fly" it to and fro in the air.
Nuthatch: Bounce your hand lightly in the air to mime a bird "hopping down the tree."
Chickadee: Open and close your beak rapidly on each "dee," moving your hand upward along with the vocal swoop on the last "dee."

Round: Divide the available singers into two or more groups and decide who will go first, second, and so on. Begin by singing the song all together once or twice; then have the first group begin the round. When the first group reaches the first asterisk in the music above, the second group comes in. Sing in two parts at first, then in three or four as your confidence grows—along with the fun!

Storybook time: Use the songbook as a storybook and point rhythmically to each bird as you sing about it.

Tingalayo

Traditional, arranged and
adapted by K. Guilmartin
Spanish words by Gerry Dignan

Moderate calypso beat

1. Tin-ga-lay-o! Come, little donkey, come, Tin-ga-lay-o!
2. Tin-ga-lay-o! Come, little donkey, come, Tin-ga-lay-o!
3. Tin-ga-lay-o! Come, little donkey, come, Tin-ga-lay-o!
4. *Tin-ga-lay-o! Ven, mi burrito, ven. Tin-ga-lay-o!*

Come, little donkey, come. My donkey walk, my donkey talk, my donkey
Come, little donkey, come. My donkey eat, my donkey sleep, my donkey
Come, little donkey, come. My donkey dance, my donkey sing, my donkey
Ven, mi burrito, ven. Burrito anda, burrito habla, burrito

eat with a knife and fork. My donkey walk, my donkey talk, my donkey
kick with his two hind feet. My donkey eat, my donkey sleep, my donkey
wear-in' a diamond ring. My donkey dance, my donkey sing, my donkey
come contenedor. Burrito anda, burrito habla, burrito

eat with a knife and fork.
kick with his two hind feet.
wear-in' a diamond ring.
come contenedor. (D.C. al Fine)

Dance and sing with the West Indian donkey who can do everything people do!

Pick up your baby, toddle with your toddler, or dance with your older child. Step to the beat, moving in a circle or winding your way through the house. Play some rattles, shakers, maracas, or a guiro as you dance and sing.

Variations: Try using your child's name instead of "Tingalayo" ("Tommy, Tommy! Dance, little Tommy, dance," or "Jenny, Jenny! Come, little Jenny, come.") Or try variations: "My Gerry walk, my Gerry talk, my Gerry eat with a cup and spoon."

Infants and toddlers: Put your baby on your hip and step to the basic beat, letting your body dip and sway easily with the music. Move from room to room, dancing playfully as you go. Stop at every mirror and let him see you both moving to the music. Lift him up high on the "Tingalayo" refrain, and then dance on the verses. When you're ready to stop, lay him down and tap his body gently to the beat as you sing the song quietly a few more times.

Recording: Guitar, bass, shakers, bongos, guiro

Betty Martin

Traditional, arranged and adapted by K. Guilmartin

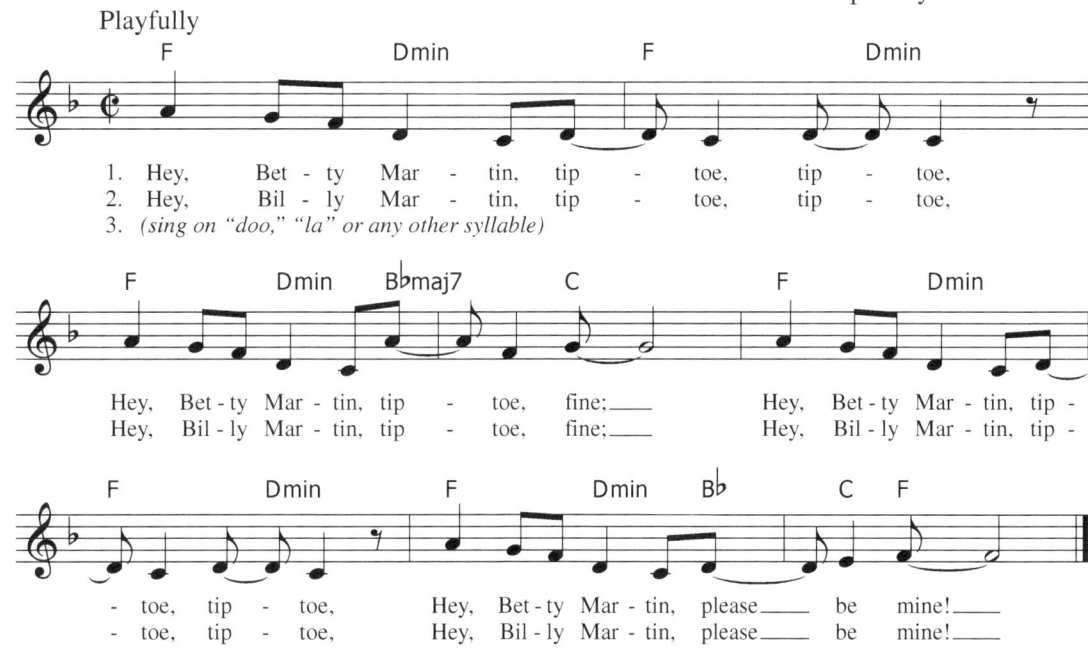

Playfully

1. Hey, Betty Martin, tip-toe, tip-toe,
2. Hey, Billy Martin, tip-toe, tip-toe,
3. *(sing on "doo," "la" or any other syllable)*

Hey, Betty Martin, tip-toe, fine;___ Hey, Betty Martin, tip-
Hey, Billy Martin, tip-toe, fine;___ Hey, Billy Martin, tip-

-toe, tip-toe, Hey, Betty Martin, please___ be mine!___
-toe, tip-toe, Hey, Billy Martin, please___ be mine!___

"Betty Martin" was popular with London theatergoers, New England fiddlers, 1812 fife and drum corpsmen, and, according to Carl Sandburg, Abraham Lincoln!

Tip-toe as you sing, or "tip-toe" with your fingers on your child's body. End with a tickle or a hug on the word "mine."

Variations: Sing your child's name instead of "Betty Martin." Substitute your name and other names, including family pets. You can even make a whole verse using just a name: "Hey, Joey, Joey, Joey, Joey, Hey, Joey, Joey, Joey, Joe," etc.

Another way to vary the song is to change the movement. Use one of your child's favorite ways to move: "Hey, Jenny Johnson, run around, run around, Hey, Jenny Johnson, run around time," etc. Repeat the movements with your child as you sing another verse on "doo" or another syllable.

Improvisation: On the recording you will hear the father's and child's voices improvise with the guitar and bass. You can try this, too. Sing on a syllable like "doo" and join in with the melody, but sing different rhythms. When you find a note that you like, keep repeating it until it sounds like you should change it. Improvisation is natural for children because it is musical play.

Recording: Guitar, bass, shakers, conga drums, triangle

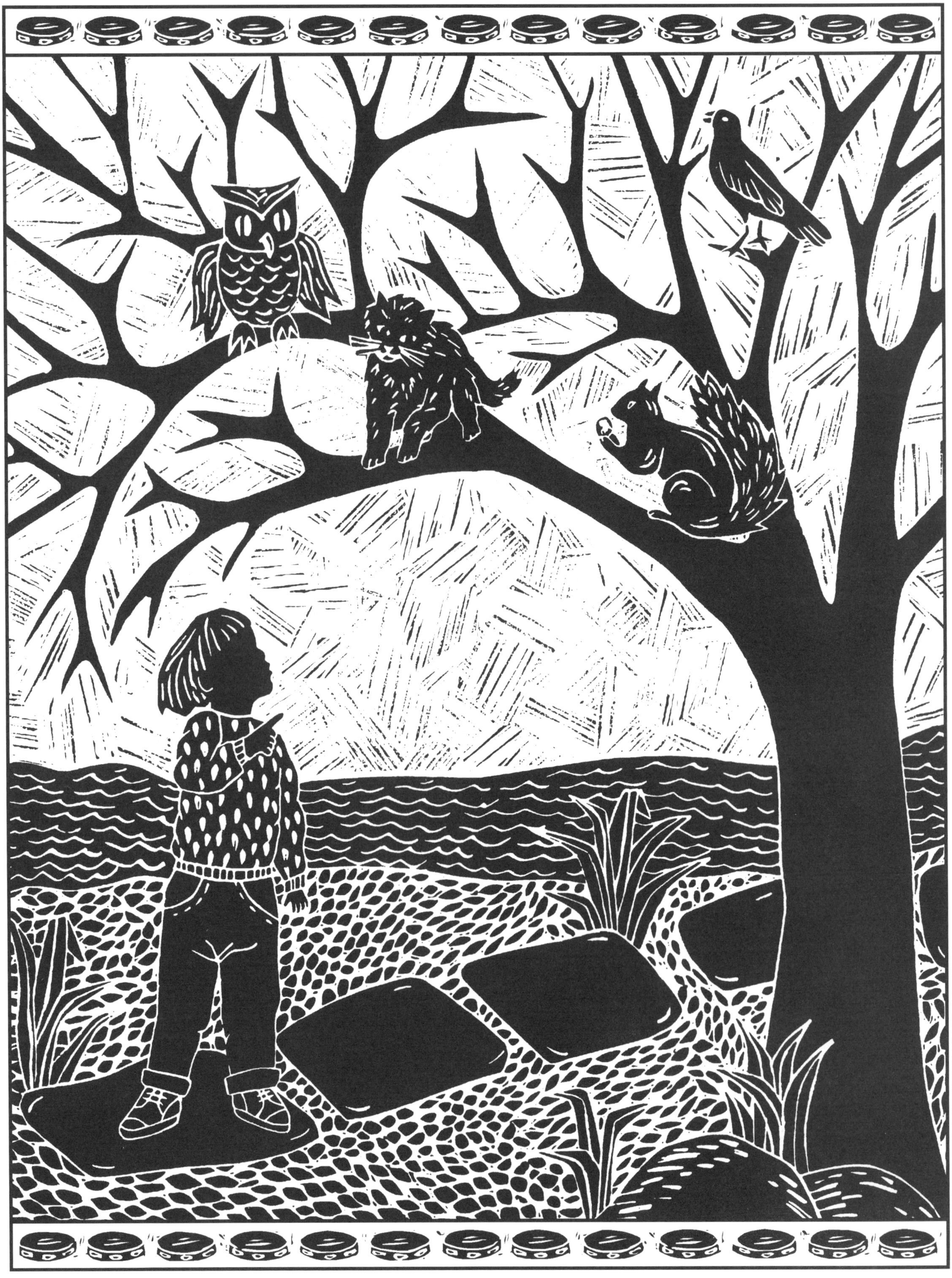

One Little Owl

Traditional, arranged and adapted
by K. Guilmartin and L. Levinowitz
Additional words by K. Guilmartin

Quietly

**Look!
What's up
in the tree?**

1. One lit-tle owl said, "whoo, whoo." Two lit-tle owls said, "whoo, whoo." Three lit-tle owls said, "whoo, whoo," as they sat in the old oak tree.
2. One lit-tle squirrel said, "sftz, sftz, sftz." Two lit-tle squirrels said, "sftz, sftz, sftz." Three lit-tle squirrels said, "sftz, sftz, sftz," as they sat in the old oak tree.
3. One lit-tle crow said, "caw, caw." Two lit-tle crows said, "caw, caw." Three lit-tle crows said, "caw, caw," as they sat in the old oak tree.
4. One lit-tle cat said, "meow, meow." Two lit-tle cats said, "meow, meow." Three lit-tle cats said, "meow, meow," as they sat in the old oak tree.

Additional verses:

5. One big mom-my said, "Hold on tight!" (*grab an imaginary branch*)
   Two big dad-dies said, "Hold on tight!" (*grab an imaginary branch*)
   Three big pa-rents said, "Hold on tight!" (*grab an imaginary branch*)
   As they sat in the old oak tree.

6. And the poor old tree said, "Oh, no!" (*raise arms like branches with palms up*)
   And the poor old tree said, . . . *etc.* . . . "All these things are sit-ting on me!"

Do characteristic movements for each animal or object as you sing about it:
  Owl: Peer wide-eyed through circles made by the thumb and index finger of each hand.
  Squirrel: Hold your hands up like squirrel "paws" in front of your chest as you chatter.
  Crow: Spread your arms out and flap them like wings.
  Cat: Rub your "paw" along your cheek, or stretch out on hands and knees.
  Oak tree: Spread your arms wide, as if they were branches.

Variations: Ask your child what else could be in the tree and what kind of sound it would make. Accept anything she suggests and sing playfully with her, making the movements of the chosen animals, machines, or other objects as best as you can. Be prepared for cows, dinosaurs, and back-hoes sitting in the tree!

Recording: Guitar, bass, bass recorder, wooden flute, ocarina, guiro, finger cymbals

Green and Blue

With delight
K. Guilmartin

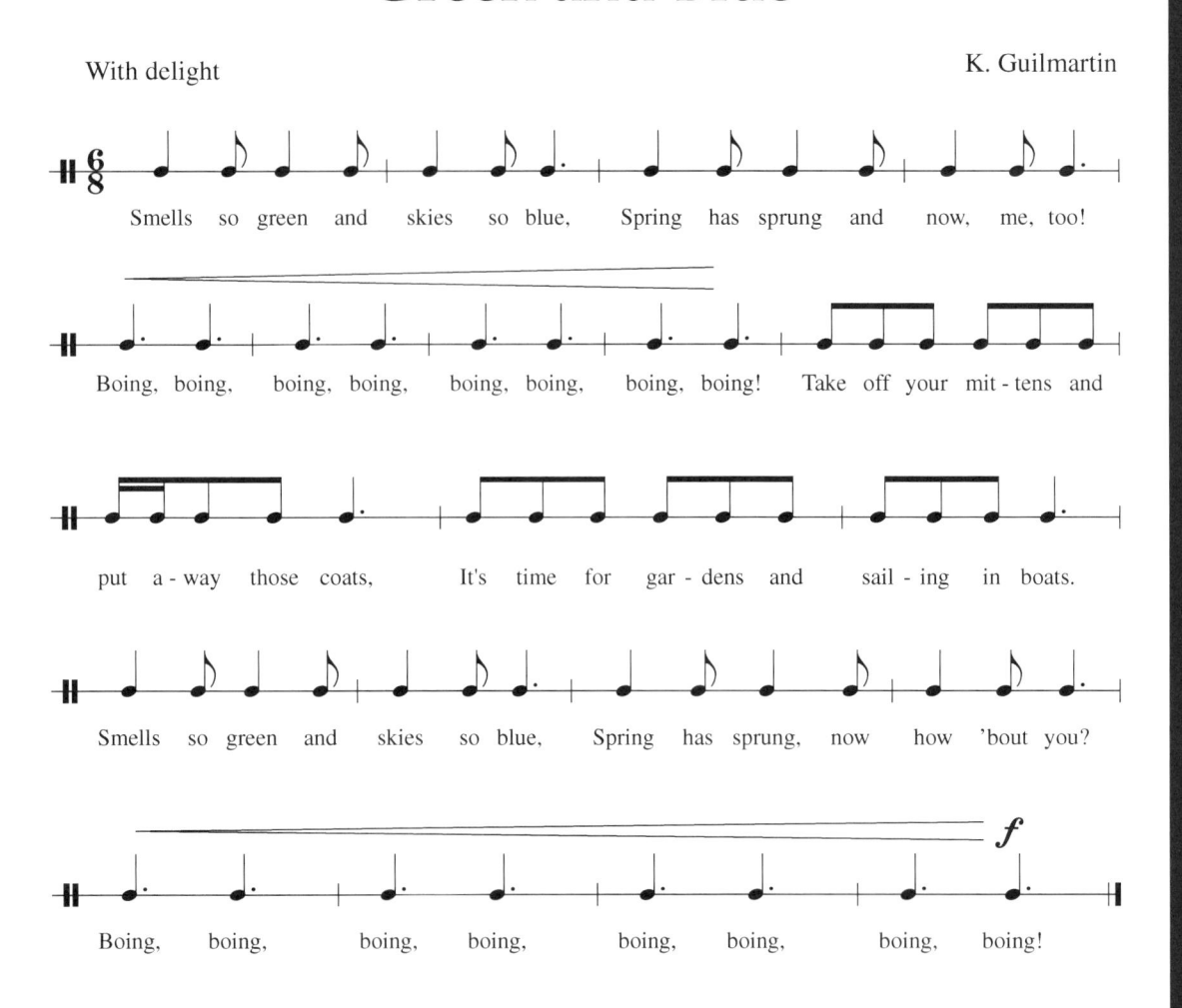

Smells so green and skies so blue, Spring has sprung and now, me, too!

Boing, boing, boing, boing, boing, boing, boing, boing! Take off your mit-tens and

put a-way those coats, It's time for gar-dens and sail-ing in boats.

Smells so green and skies so blue, Spring has sprung, now how 'bout you?

f

Boing, boing, boing, boing, boing, boing, boing, boing!

Celebrate the smells, the colors —and the rhythms!— of spring.

Think spring, imagine being a child again, take a big breath of fresh air, and say the chant. Make up simple movements to go with the words. For example:

"Smells so green": Gesture with your hands as if smelling a bouquet of flowers, then make a similar, larger gesture to the sky.
"Spring has sprung": Make your hands jump on "sprung," then tap your chest on "me, too!"
"Boing, boing": Bounce your hands in the air as if they were flowers popping up out of the ground here, there, everywhere!
"Take off those mittens": Mime the actions.
"It's time for gardens": "Dig" in the garden and "sail" your hand over the waves.
"Spring has sprung, now how 'bout you?": As above, make your hands jump on "sprung," then gesture to your child or pick her up. Bounce your hands higher and higher on the "boing" sounds, or get up and jump!

Rhythm: The triple meter rhythm feels like a waltz, with three small beats for every large one. You can experience this if you sway or rock as you speak the words, shifting your weight from one foot to the other.

Hey Ya Na

Traditional
Native American (Apache)

With a strong beat

E (no 3rd) throughout

Hey ya na, Hey ya na, O ha— le ya na ya.

Hey ya hey ya, Hey— ya na, O ha— le ya na ya.

Dance to the heartbeat of the drum.

Dance as you sing, connecting through your feet to the earth. Native American dancing emphasizes this connection, so bend over slightly at the waist, and focus more on the movement in your feet and legs than in your arms, torso, or head.

Large movement: The drums on the recording beat in a classic "heartbeat" pattern: strong-weak, strong-weak. Keep this feeling as you try some types of Native American dance steps. For example, walk deliberately, placing your toe on the floor on the strong beat, then lower the heel to the floor on the weak beat. Or move sideways, to the right, step-close, step-close. As your dancing becomes more confident, try some dancing spins: hop on one foot while twirling around in a small circle. For all of these steps, keep your arms loose and your body bent slightly toward the earth.

Instrument play: Get out your percussion instruments and play. Rattles, maracas, drums, jingle bells, and shakers all go well with this song. Some of the family can play drums while others dance; then switch.

Note: The words in "Hey Ya Na" have no literal meaning. They are neutral syllables or "vocables" chosen for their sound and rhythmic qualities.

Recording: Drums, shakers, bells

See the Pony Galloping

Traditional, arranged
by K. Guilmartin

INTRO
At a gallop!

VERSE

See the po-ny gal-lop-ing, gal-lop-ing, down the coun-try lane!

Gradually slower and quieter

lane! See the po-ny com-ing home, all tired out,

all tired out, all tired out.

Pretend to be a pony enjoying the sounds and rhythms of galloping—until you fall asleep!

You can start by sitting with your child on your lap, bouncing him to the beat of the music. Make "clip-clop" sounds by clucking your tongue in the galloping rhythm of the song; then sing. As the music slows down, lie down together to "sleep" for a minute, then sit up suddenly, perhaps with a "neigh," and start all over again. You can also get up and gallop around the room or yard.

Variations: Hold a toy horse or stuffed animal and make it "gallop" as you whinny and sing. Use your full vocal range to play with the animal sounds. When you see a pony—in a pasture, on TV, or in a book—try singing this song.

Note: This song is playful and full of contrasts. It also provides important musical experiences: *ritardando* (slowing down), *diminuendo* (getting quiet), and *sforzando* (being suddenly loud).

Recording: Guitar, bass, harmonica, wood block

Wedding Dance

Traditional, arranged and adapted by K. Guilmartin

Dance and sing to this klezmer-style arrangement of a Hasidic tune.

Ya da yat dat da, Ya da da yat dat da, (etc.)

Gradually slower

Sing and step to the beat of the music, accenting the strong beats by stomping into the floor. Gather everyone together and dance in a circle, moving to the right and left, in and out.

Infants: Lay your infant down so he can see you; then dance to the music, perhaps waving a colorful scarf. You can also help him feel the music by tapping his body in time and/or dancing with him.

Instrument play: Shake wrist bells lightly or wear them on wrists or ankles. Try leading with a tambourine, as Israeli folk dance leaders do; then pass the leadership to others by passing the tambourine.

Tonality: "Wedding Dance" is in a unique tonality called "Ahava Raba" which means "Love a lot." Music for weddings and bar mitzvahs are often written in this tonality.

Recording: Guitar, bass, soprano sax, tambourine, drums

Tricks with Sticks

K. Guilmartin

INTRO

With a beat (♪♪ = ♪♪)

("scat" ad lib)

Choo chik - ka choo chik - ka choo choo choo choo.

Boom chik - ka boom chik - ka boom boom boom.

Skit - tle - y - up - pa doo - dah, a - ding dong ding.

Scoob - a doob - a doob - a, a - bing bong bing.

VERSE 1

Hey, ev - 'ry - bod - y, lis - ten to me, watch real close and then you'll see

how to do some nif - ty tricks, pick up your sticks and go like this:

CHORUS

Ba da dum__ ba dum bum bum bum, ba da dum__ ba dum dum.

ba da dum__ ba dum bum bum bum, ba da dum__ ba dum dum.

Ba da dum__ ba dum bum bum bum, ba da dum__ ba dum dum.

VERSE 2

Well, How do you do? and What a - bout that? Bark goes the dog, me - ow goes the cat!

sing CHORUS

For nifty tricks, pick up your sticks!

VERSE 3

I wonder how many things I can do, es-pec-ially when I'm hav-in' fun play-in' with you!
sing CHORUS

("scat" ad lib)
Pom pom - pa rump - a pom pom, (Sha-)
boom sha - boom___ dee yad - da da - da da - da, Sha -
bop bop - pa loo bop ba - lop bam boom,
Skit - tle - y - up - pa doo - wop a - zzz - zoom!
sing CHORUS

Optional drone harmony:

Ba da dum___ ba dum bum bum bum, *etc.*

Optional harmonies:

Ba da dum___ ba dum *etc.*

Get out the rhythm sticks, wooden spoons, or dowel rods and tap them to the beat.

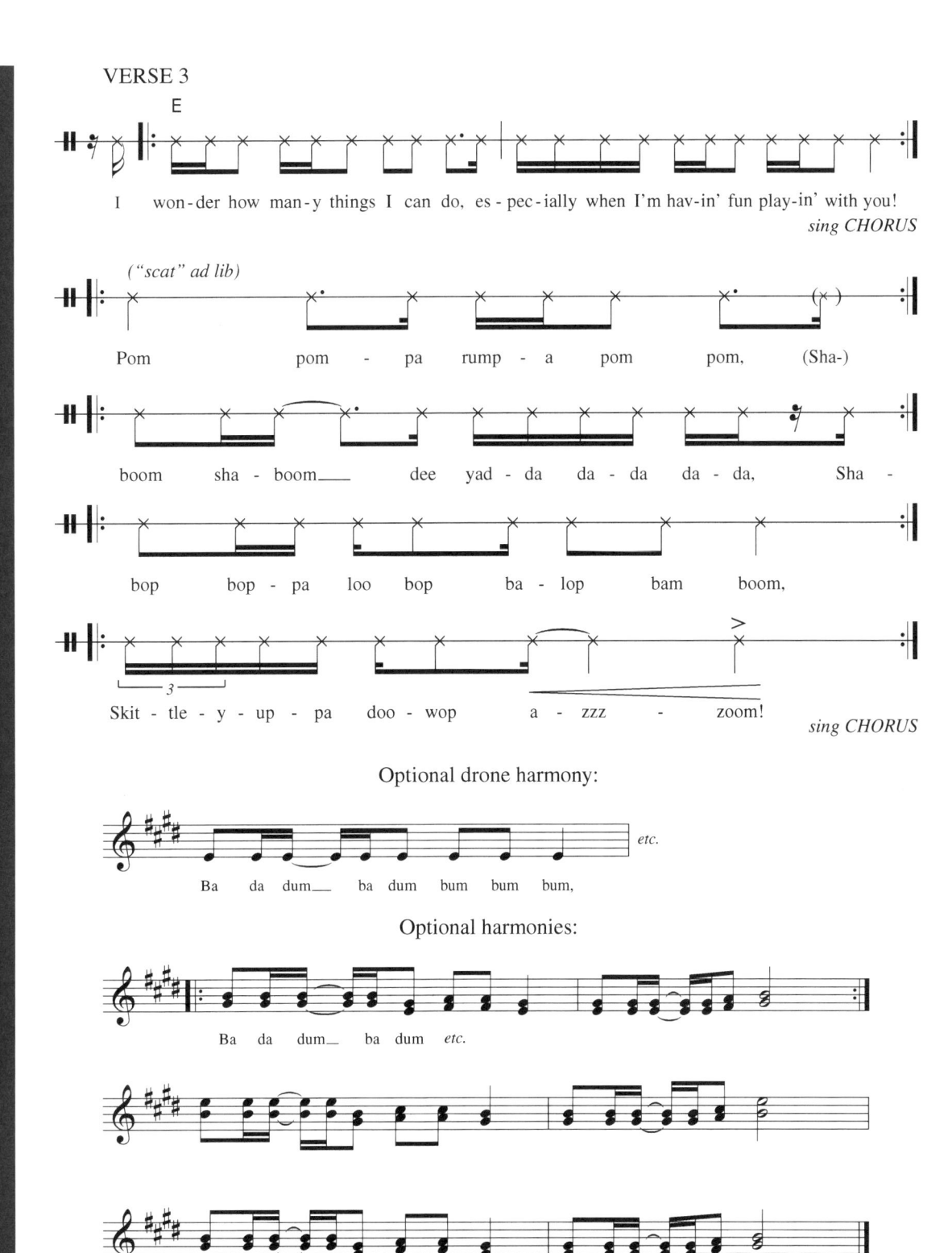

Verse variations: Echo the scat lines as the singers do on the recording. Then create your own by making short, silly phrases of words or sounds that can be echoed by others in your family.

Mouth music: Many cultures have some kind of "mouth music"—musical syllables that don't carry specific meaning. North American traditions include Native American chant, "doo-wop" (1950s rock 'n' roll), and the rhythmic syllables known in jazz as "scat."

Recording: Guitar, bass, conga drums, rhythm sticks, shaker, maracas, cowbell

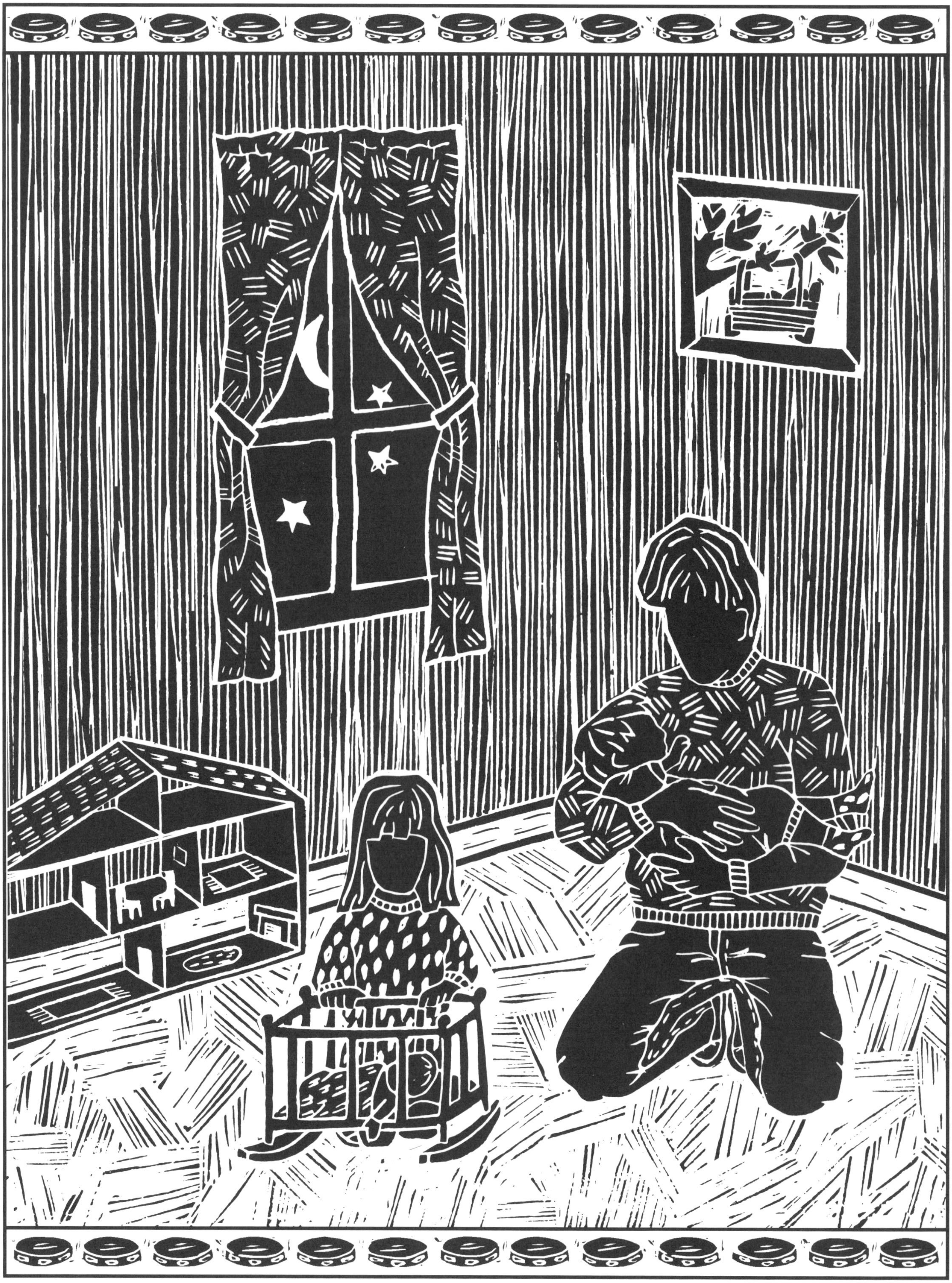

Cradle Song

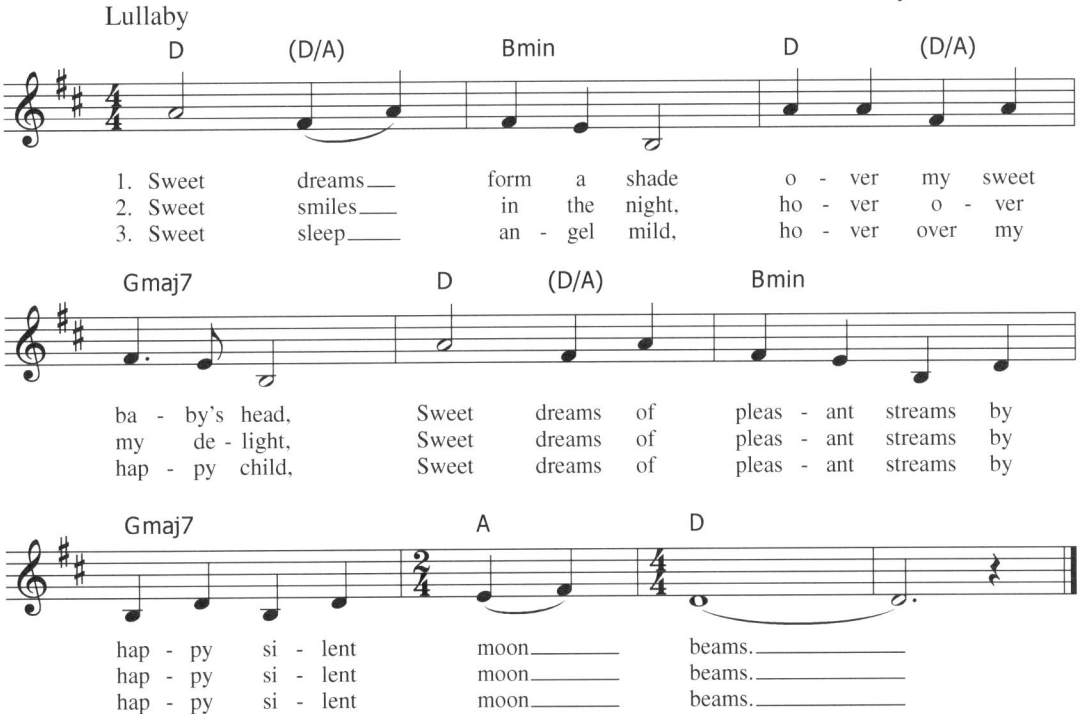

Words by William Blake
Music by K. Guilmartin

Cuddle, rock, and sing of sweet dreams and moonbeams.

Lullaby

1. Sweet dreams form a shade o - ver my sweet ba - by's head, Sweet dreams of pleas - ant streams by hap - py si - lent moon beams.
2. Sweet smiles in the night, ho - ver o - ver my de - light, Sweet dreams of pleas - ant streams by hap - py si - lent moon beams.
3. Sweet sleep an - gel mild, ho - ver over my hap - py child, Sweet dreams of pleas - ant streams by hap - py si - lent moon beams.

Sing or hum this lullaby when you want to help your child settle—at naptime, bedtime, riding on a plane, or when he's not feeling well. Sing gently, rocking and caressing him. With enough repetition, music has the power to soothe and quiet even the most active child. Invite an older child to join in as you sing to his pets or dolls.

Rocking chair and cradle: Rock and sing, moving gently in rhythm with the music. When it's time to put your child in bed, keep singing while you get her ready and tuck her in. Then sing or hum one more verse quietly, close to her, so she can sense your breathing and feel your voice.

Songbook illustration: Look at the illustration on the opposite page with your child. Who is the little girl rocking the cradle? Can you find another cradle in the picture? Many children are fascinated by the moon and stars. As you sing the song, point out the moon in the book or in the window.

Note: The words of this song are from *Songs of Innocence* (1789), a collection of poems and paintings by William Blake, an eighteenth century poet.

Recording: Piano

Tambourine Jam

"Get your instrument and play along!"

K. Guilmartin

A high-point of Music Together classes is the jam session we call the "play-along."

In a play-along, everyone, infant to grandparent, chooses an instrument and plays along with a recording or with live musicians. Suggestion: Before you get out the instruments, try listening to the play-along a few times while you move or dance to the rhythms with your child.

Keep your own collection of real and "found" instruments handy in a drawer or basket, so you can pull them out easily for a play-along—or get out the pots and pans! Everybody plays something. If you haven't touched that clarinet since high school or college, why not get it out and try? Your example of participation means so much more to your child than performing the "right notes."

As you become familiar with "Tambourine Jam," stop, start, and accent with the flow of the music. If you exaggerate these moments somewhat, even toddlers may notice and follow you! Just repeatedly set the example and see what happens.

This song is also good for dancing or free movement, or you may want to move and play an instrument at the same time. If children do this, just make sure the instrument is safe for movement.

Even older children may not be developmentally ready to perform with accuracy and may prefer to use instruments more creatively than "correctly." Some may just hold the instrument while they dance or watch others. Appreciate any form of participation, even just wide-eyed attention!

Note: The unusual tambourine-like sounds on the recording are made by a "rik," a Middle Eastern tambourine with large jingles. Rik performance techniques include playing patterns on the jingles as much as on the skin head.

Recording: Piano, guitar, bass, harmonica, drums, shakers, bodhran (Irish frame drum), rik

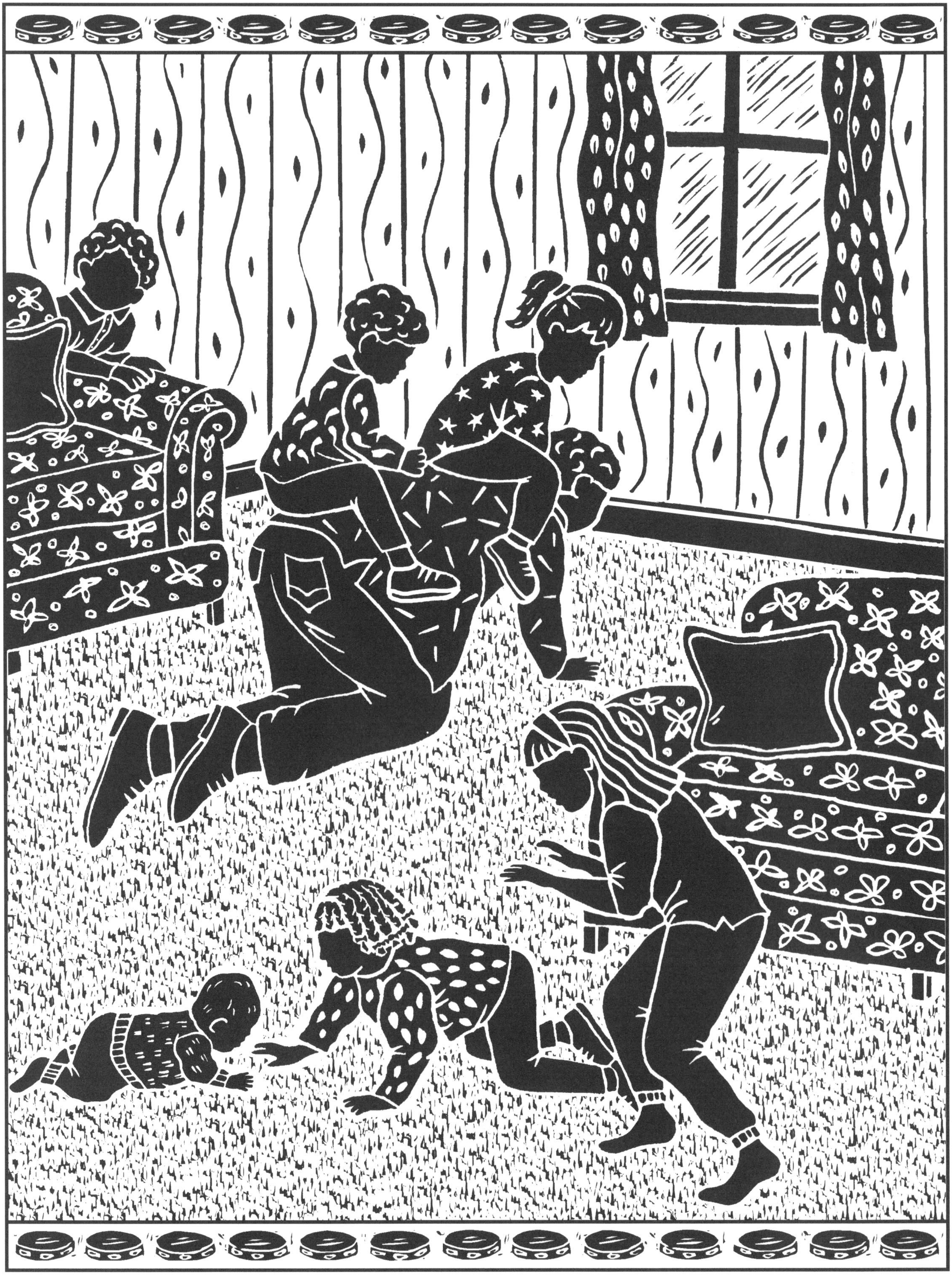

Sneakin' 'Round the Room

K. Guilmartin

Sneak, strut, waltz, and boogie in your living room!

VARIATIONS

1. Swing — Doo doo doo doo doo ___ etc.
2. Waltz — La la la la la etc.
3. Boogie Woogie — Scoo-bie doo-bie doo-bie doo-wah ___ etc., then D.C. al Coda

Boo!

Use the recording to learn the four basic movements and singing styles: sneak (quietly, with drama and suspense), walk (hip, cool, with attitude), dance (waltz, spin, sway), and boogie (jazzy).

Songbook illustration: Sing the tune in different ways for different people in the picture. For example, sing "doo" for the girl on her knees and "waaah" for the baby. Sing in a deeper voice for the dad, a scary voice for the big girl, and very quietly for the boy hiding behind the chair.

Note: The fermatas (⌒) in the music indicate when to "hold" the notes to build suspense. It's also fun to "freeze" your movement while you hold your singing note on each of the fermatas.

Recording: Piano, bass, pennywhistle, drums

Hippity, Happity, Hoppity

Doug Morris

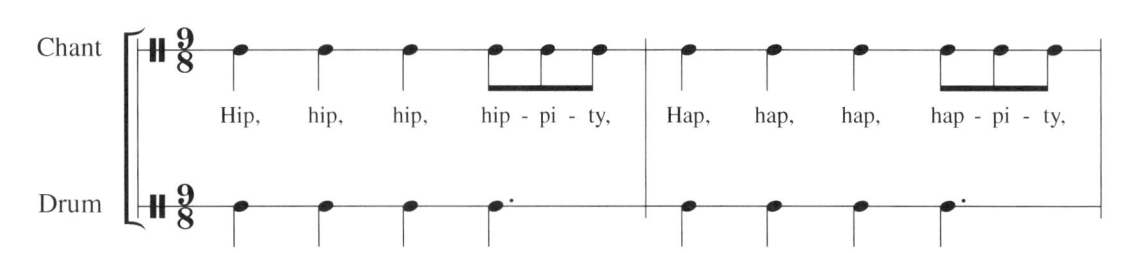

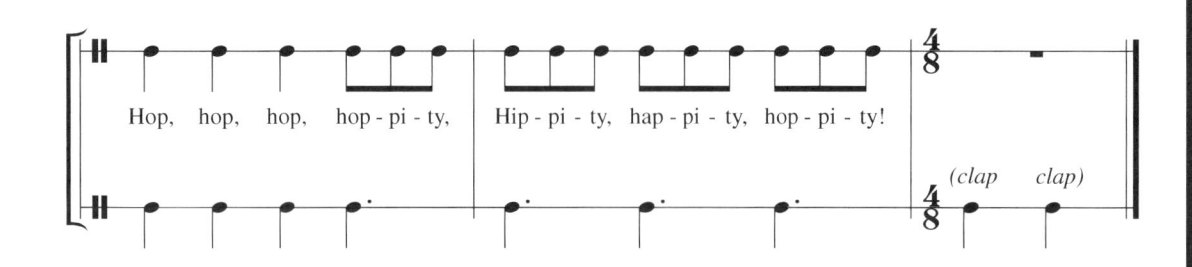

Energetically

[Chant and Drum notation in 9/8 time, transitioning to 4/8]

Hip, hip, hip, hip-pi-ty, Hap, hap, hap, hap-pi-ty,
Hop, hop, hop, hop-pi-ty, Hip-pi-ty, hap-pi-ty, hop-pi-ty! (clap clap)

Clap 'n' tap along with the snazzy, jazzy rhythm of this chant.

Get to know this interesting rhythm by saying the chant along with the recording as you move with your child in rhythmic ways. After a while you'll find yourself spontaneously thinking or saying the chant without the help of the recording!

Rhythm note: Most music in Western culture tends to group either two or three beats together, creating what we call either duple meter (like a march) or triple meter (like a waltz). This chant, however, combines groups of two *and* three beats together in one phrase, providing a wonderful sense of drive. Each phrase contains nine microbeats, grouped into pulses of twos and threes as follows:

1-2 **1**-2 **1**-2 **1** - 2 - 3   **1**-2 **1**-2 **1**-2 **1** - 2 - 3   **1**-2 **1**-2 **1**-2 **1** - 2 - 3
Hip, hip, hip, hip-pi-ty,   **Hap, hap, hap, hap**-pi-ty,   **Hop, hop, hop, hop**-pi-ty,

1 - 2 - 3   **1** - 2 - 3   **1** - 2 - 3   **1**-2   **1**-2
Hip-pi-ty,   **hap**-pi-ty,   **hop**-pi-ty!   (clap)   (clap)

Try putting this unequal rhythm into your body by tapping your legs on the short (duple) beats, and tapping your head on the long (triple) beats: leg-leg-leg-head, leg-leg-leg-head. You can also try tapping on the twos and making a circular motion on the threes to illustrate the different size beats. This kind of uneven grouping is common in world music, but some Western adults may find it unusual or challenging at first. For a child, early experience with a chant like "Hippity, Happity, Hoppity" will make this kind of rhythm as accessible as any other and will expand her rhythmic vocabulary.

Recording: Claves, shakers

Pawpaw Patch

Traditional, arranged and adapted by K. Guilmartin

**Where's Susie?
Let's go find her!**

Brightly

1. Where, oh where, oh where is Su-sie? Where, oh where, oh where is Su-sie?
2. Come on kids, let's go find her, Come on kids, let's go find her,

Where, oh where, oh where is Su-sie? Way down yon-der in the paw-paw patch.
Come on kids, let's go find her, Way down yon-der in the paw-paw patch.

Fine

3. Pick-in' up paw-paws, put 'em in your pock-et, Pick-in' up paw-paws, put 'em in your pock-et, Pick-in' up paw-paws, put 'em in your pock-et,

Way down yon-der in the paw-paw patch.

D.C. al Fine

Act out the song by moving rhythmically with motions that suit the words. Pretend to shield your eyes from the sun as you search for "Susie," then point (on the beat) to an imaginary pawpaw patch, gesture for the "kids" to come along, and end by happily picking pawpaws.

Variations: Sing when something's lost—"Where, oh where, oh where are my car keys?" and "Come on, Paul, help me find them."

Hide-and-seek: Young children love games of hide-and-seek. Everyone takes turns hiding while the rest of the family sings "where, oh where, oh where is ____," and so on. If younger children want company hiding, fit two names to the tune!

Infants and toddlers: Hide something small, like a rattle, under a blanket while your baby watches. Sing, "Where, oh where, oh where's the rattle?" Then pull it out and sing, "Here, oh here, oh here's the rattle," shaking it to the beat as you sing. Hide the rattle and sing again, and see what happens.

History: A pawpaw is a large fruit that looks like a mango and grows on trees with big, droopy, tropical-looking leaves. It tastes like banana-strawberry custard and is found in 26 states.

Recording: Guitar, bass, tambourine

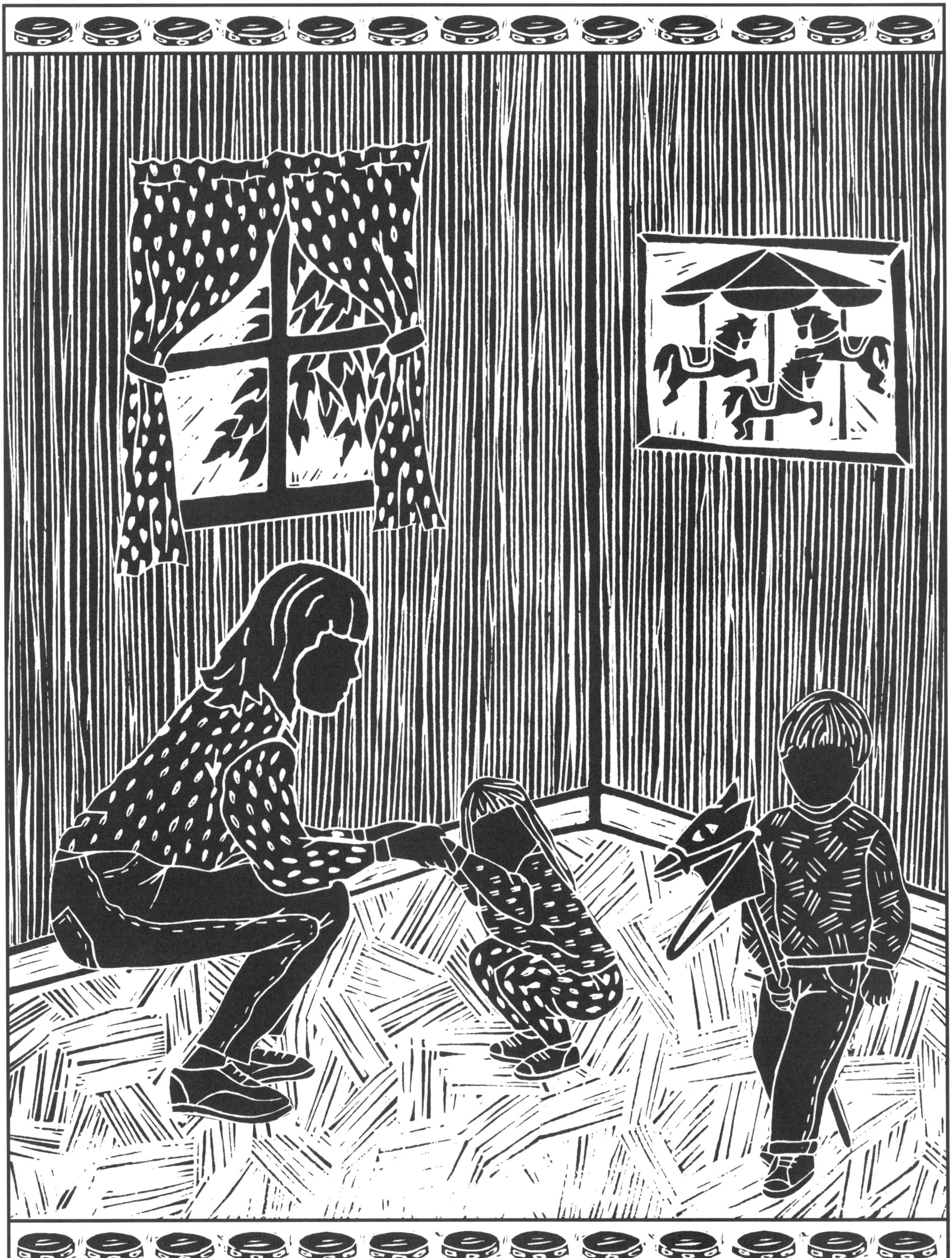

Merry-Go-Round

Lynn Lobban

Dizzily

Ride the horse up and down, around and around!

1. Mer - ry - go - round, mer - ry - go - round, a - round and a - round and a - round. Mer - ry - go - round, mer - ry - go - round, a - round and a - round and a - round. The hors - es go up and then they go down, a - round and a - round and a - round. The hors - es go up and then they go down, a - round and a - round and a - round.

2. Diz - zy go 'round, diz - zy go 'round, a - round and a - round and a - round. Diz - zy go 'round, diz - zy go 'round, a - round and a - round and a - round.

3. Mer - ry - go - round, mer - ry - go - round, a - round and a - round and a - round. Mer - ry - go - round, mer - ry - go - round, a - round and a - round and a - round. I ride the horse up and ride the horse down, a - round and a - round and a - round. I ride the horse up and ride the horse down, a - round and a - round and a - round. *(D.C. al Coda)*

round and a - round and a - round and a - round and a - round!

Move your arms in a circle in time to the music as you sing this song. When you sing about the horses going up and down, try lifting up and lowering your child. You can even move around the room as if you were horses on a merry-go-round, moving up and down as you circle around.

Songbook illustration: Look at the illustration on the opposite page as you sing the song with your child. Hold the last note (the "resting tone") and *sing* some questions to her on this note. For example, "What is the little boy doing?" or "What do you see in the picture on the wall?"

Recording: Guitar, bass, MIDI calliope, wood block, bell tree

Secrets

Linda Betlejeski, K. Guilmartin
and L. Levinowitz

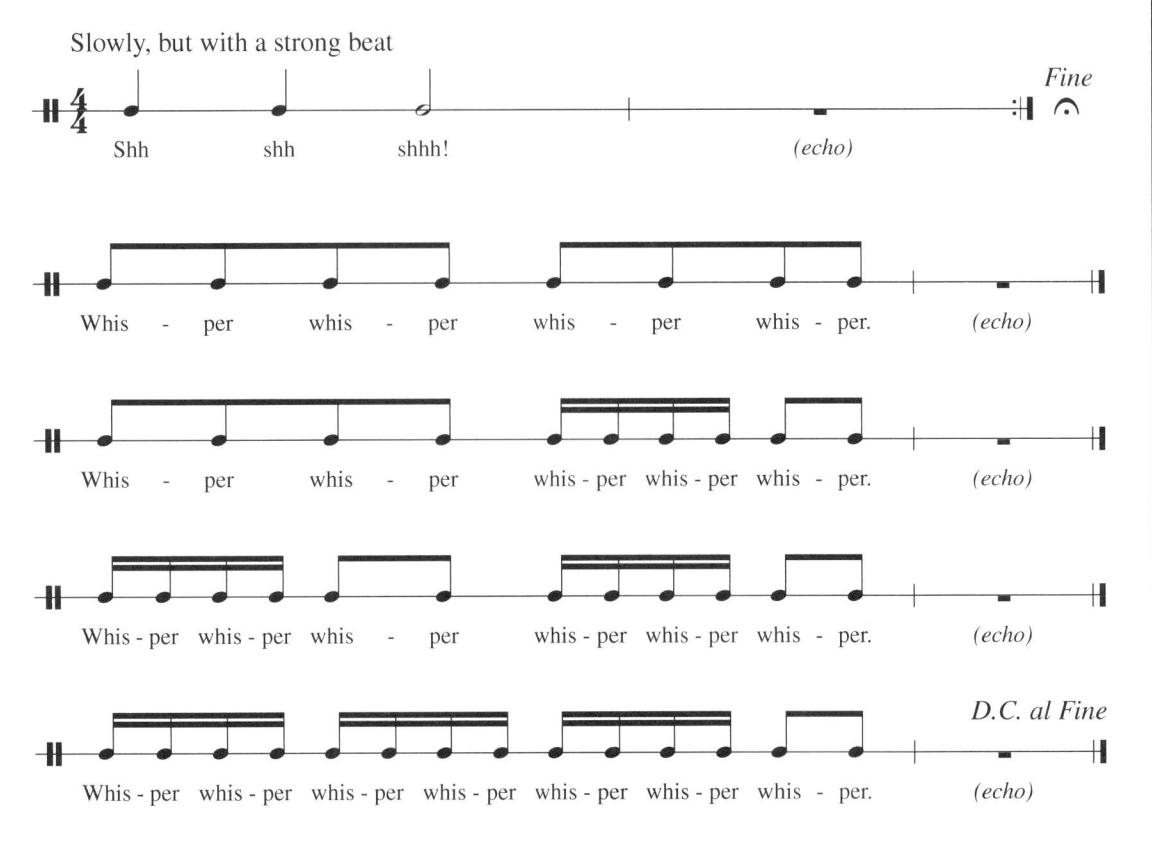

Slowly, but with a strong beat

Shh shh shhh! (echo) *Fine*

Whis - per whis - per whis - per whis - per. (echo)

Whis - per whis - per whis - per whis - per whis - per. (echo)

Whis - per whis - per whis - per whis - per whis - per whis - per. (echo)

D.C. al Fine

Whis - per whis - per whis - per whis - per whis - per whis - per whis - per. (echo)

**Shhhhh!
I've got a secret.**

Sit close and whisper the chant to your child. (Be sure you start slowly enough to be able to say the last line!) After they have learned it, older children may be able to answer with the echo (as heard on the CD). If your child is younger, model the echo with the help of an older child or another adult, or simply repeat each phrase in an even quieter voice.

Variations: First become comfortable with the form of this chant: a phrase followed by its echo, then a different phrase followed by its echo. Then make up a new phrase and whisper it rhythmically in a hushed voice. Try using two-syllable words like "se-cret" or "ec-ho." Try words that are especially interesting or exciting for your child: "pre-sent" or "ice cream." Use this chant the next time you want to tell your child about a special surprise.

Rhythm note: This song provides a structured experience of different levels of beat, especially macrobeat (the basic beat), microbeat (twice as fast), and the next level of diminution (four times as fast). See the glossary for definitions of macrobeat and microbeat.

Rhythm development: Children benefit from hearing the chant many times and freely experimenting with saying it their way, even if that differs from the "correct" version. When your child's development allows her to echo each phrase, it will be interesting for you to see if she keeps a steady beat, even though the words get very fast. When she can keep the beat steadily throughout and echo patterns accurately, she has probably achieved basic rhythm competence.

Ding Dong, Ding Dong

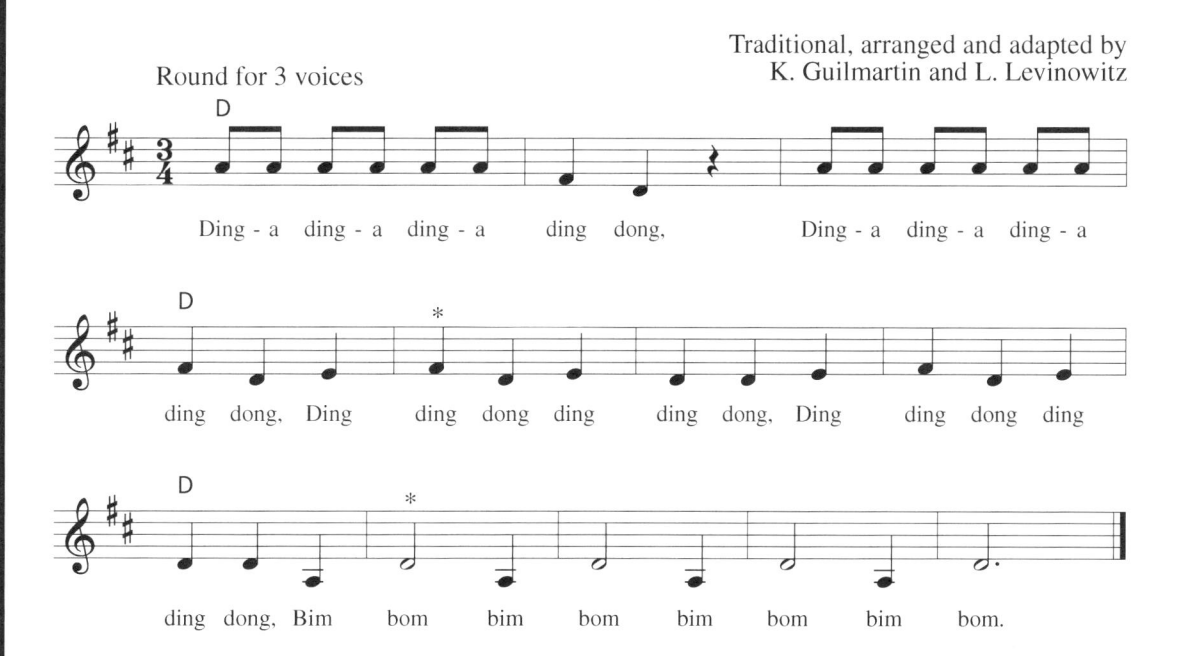

Round for 3 voices

Traditional, arranged and adapted by
K. Guilmartin and L. Levinowitz

Ding - a ding - a ding - a ding dong, Ding - a ding - a ding - a ding dong, Ding ding dong ding ding dong, Ding ding dong ding ding dong, Bim bom bim bom bim bom bim bom.

To create a round, additional voices can begin singing when the first voice reaches the asterisk (*).

Sing the sound of ringing bells.

Sing and sway to the macrobeat, following the three-beat feel of the music. The tempo and feel match the way children rock back and forth, shifting their weight naturally from one foot to the other.

Singing a round: When your family knows the song well, divide into two groups with some stronger singers in each group. One group starts the round, and the second group enters after one phrase, as indicated by the asterisks in the music and heard on the recording. This can be especially rewarding for older children or adults who may discover they can "hold their own part" for the first time; but remember that getting "lost" is all part of the fun! For a three-part round, a third group enters after group two sings the first phrase.

Bell play: Play along with any bells you can find—jingle bells, school bells, bells on charm bracelets—as well as objects with ringing, bell-like, metallic sounds—full key rings or kitchen equipment. For some children, this concrete expression of bells will be fascinating. Another day, pretend to ring imaginary hand bells or pull on a big rope to ring a cathedral bell.

Learning rhythm: It is important for young children to experience rhythm through movement, so instead of just singing this song, move to it as well. This can help your child establish a strong sense of pulse during the years when he can develop this most easily.

Recording: Celesta

This 'n' That

K. Guilmartin

Cuban feel

1, 6. Na na na na na, Na na na na na.
2. Dance with me like this, Dance with me like that.
3. *Va - mos a bai - lar a - sí, Va - mos a bai - lar a - sí.*
4. Move your hips like this, Move your hips like that.
5. Can you go like this? Can you go like that?
7. Sing a song like this, Sing a song like that.
8. *Va - mos a can - tar a - sí, Va - mos a can - tar a - sí.*

Na na na na na, Na na na na na.
Dance with me like this, Dance with me like that.
Va - mos a bai - lar a - sí, Va - mos a bai - lar a - sí.
Move your hips like this, Move your hips like that. *(to Interlude)*
We can go like this. We can go like that.
Sing a song like this, Sing a song like that.
Va - mos a can - tar a - sí, Va - mos a can - tar a - sí. *(to Interlude)*

INTERLUDE
(After verse 8, vamp *ad lib. al Fine*)

(sing on "la")

Fine

Join in on the dancing fun!

Make up movements or just let loose and dance the mambo! Carry little ones or just let them watch. Everyone sings the "na na" or "la la" verses. Then try doing the following kinds of interactions:

Dance with me like this: Leader models contrasting movements (right/left, up/down, slow/fast).
Move your hips like this: Find different ways to move your hips, or move other parts of your body like your arms or shoulders.
Can you go like this: Leader models and followers sing "we can go like this" as they do it.
Sing a song like this (*): At the asterisks, followers answer by singing "na, na, na" as on the recording, perhaps using some of the harmonies presented.

Spanish translation: *Vamos a bailar asi* means "let's dance like this." Similarly, *vamos a cantar asi* means "let's sing like this." In Spanish, there is no difference between the words "this" and "that."

Recording: Piano, bass, conga drums, timbales, cowbell, claves

Scarborough Fair

Traditional, arranged
by K. Guilmartin

A favorite of many generations— pass it along to your children.

Lyrically

Are you goin' to Scarborough Fair? Parsley, sage, rosemary and thyme. Remember me to one who lives there, For he *(or "she")* once was a true love of mine.

Rhythmic movement helps children connect with slow, quiet music. Sway and sing while you hold your child close, moving your whole torso so she will feel you move and breathe.

Large movement: Toddlers can stand on your feet as you rock side-to-side. Older children can rock independently or sway with a partner (dolls or stuffed animals can also be partners). Get out scarves or pieces of cloth, and let them flow with you as you move to the music, using your whole body.

Singing in harmony: If you enjoy singing harmony, try singing the harmony heard on the last verse of the recording. You can learn it by singing along with the CD or by reading the small cue notes in the music. You can also create a simple drone (a held or repeated note) harmony by singing the resting tone (B, the song's first note) all the way through the song, while someone else sings the melody. Note the lovely dissonance on the word "there."

Lullaby: Sing this familiar folk song to your child as he settles for sleep.

Guitar: Guitarists may find it easier to put the capo on the second fret and play in A minor.

Recording: Guitar, bass, pennywhistle

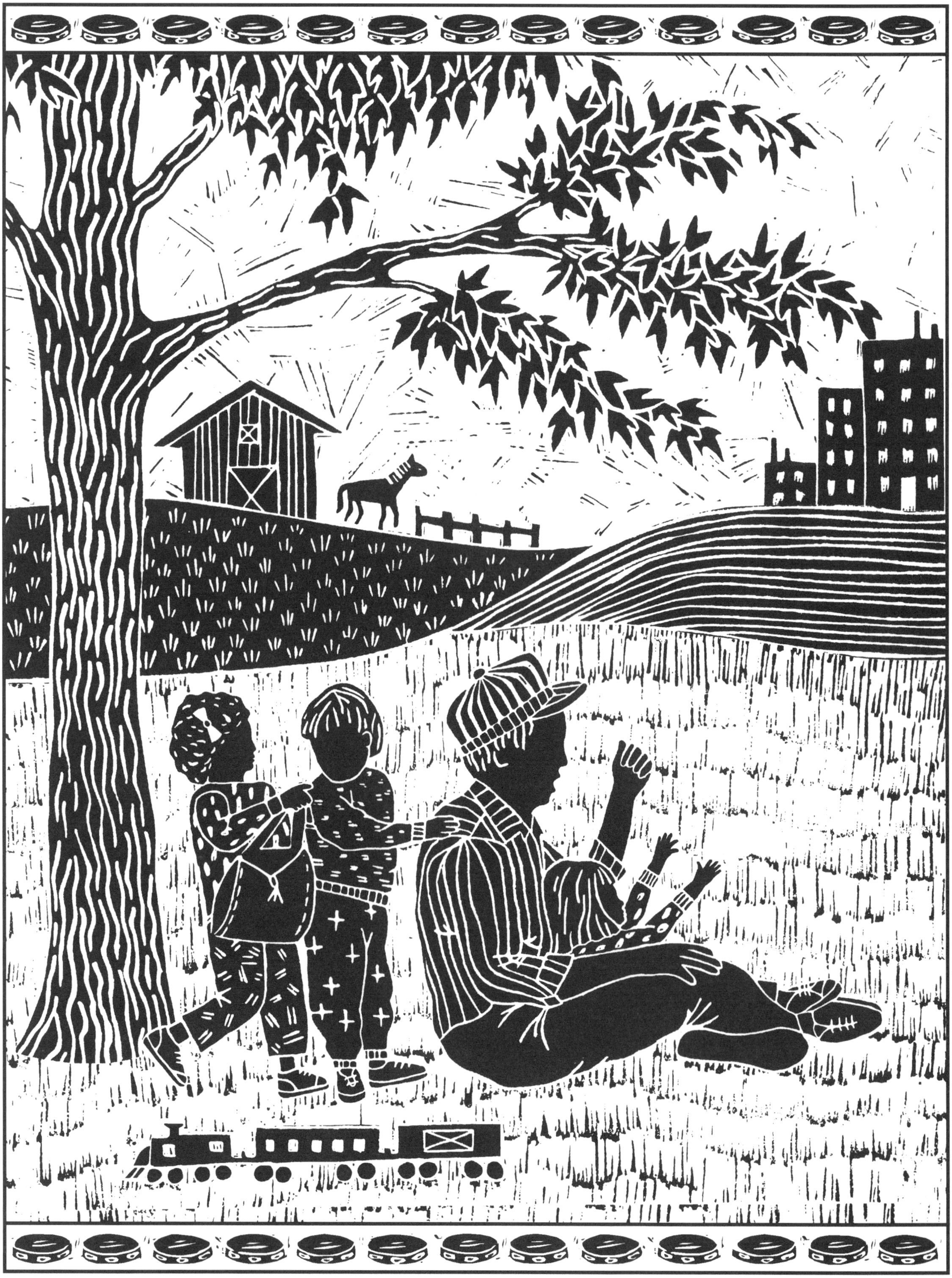

Good News

Traditional African-American spiritual, arranged with additional lyrics by K. Guilmartin

Let's go—but don't leave me behind!

With a beat (♫ = ♩♪)

1. Good news! Char-i-ot's a-com-in', — Good news!
2. *(sing on "doo")*
3. Beep! Beep! Bus __ is a-com-in', __ *etc.*
4. Toot! Toot! Train __ is a-com-in', __ *etc.*

Char-i-ot's a-com-in', __ Good news! Char-i-ot's a-com-in',

1.-3. Fine — don't leave me be-hind.

4. hind.

(optional: sing melody on "doo")

Choo choo choo choo choo choo choo choo *etc.*

D.C. al Fine

Sing the song as written, moving around the room as if you were on a chariot, bus, or train. People of all ages can enjoy making train sounds, forming a train, and following the leader around the house.

Traveling: Older children will enjoy singing about different ways they travel—car, train, plane, trucks, and boats. Imaginary travel could be fun, too—pterodactyl, magic carpet, space ship, fire truck, etc.

Singing in harmony: Sing the "choo-choo" vocal harmony which follows the train verse. Learn it by singing along with the singers on the recording; then sing it without the recording.

Recording: Guitar, bass, harmonica, drums, tambourine

Raisins and Almonds

Traditional Yiddish folk song,
arranged by K. Guilmartin

Lullaby

To my little one's cradle in the night comes a little goat snow-y and white. The goat will trot to the mar-ket, while moth-er her watch does keep, bring-ing back rai-sins and al-monds.

1. Sleep, my lit-tle one, sleep.
2. Sleep, my lit-tle one, sleep.

A rich and warm traditional melody brings sweet dreams.

This is a lovely tune to sing anytime, anywhere, but it is especially fine as a lullaby. Standing, or rocking in a chair, sway gently back and forth to the beat as you sing "to Elizabeth's cradle" or "to my little John's cradle." Adapt the words and rhythm to your child's name; then hum the melody or sing on "la," "noo," or another syllable.

Infants: Sing to your infant in a relaxed way. If you leave a little silence between repetitions and if your child is vocal, she may spontaneously make her own "lullaby" sounds. Imitate the sounds she makes, then change them slightly and see her response. She may change her sounds, too, or may just listen.

Songbook: Make music part of your ritual before bedtime or naptime by using the songbook as a storybook. Page through the book together, looking at the pictures and singing a little bit of each song you know. Your model will help your child want to learn to sing and read music books, too.

When grandparents, babysitters, and other caregivers put your child to bed, give them the book and ask them to follow your bedtime ritual. After a while, your older child may want to page through the book on his own, singing the song or parts of the songs to himself. Children may also enjoy paging through the book while listening to the CD—the book's song order follows the CD song order, and this lovely song is at the end.

Recording: Guitar, bass

Goodbye, So Long, Farewell

K. Guilmartin

Jazz waltz

1. Good-bye, so long, fare-well, my friends, good-bye, so long, fare-well. We'll see you soon a-gain, my friends, so good-bye, so long, fare-well.
2. Good-bye to *(name)*, good-bye to *(different name)*, good-bye, so long, fare-well. Good-bye to ev-'ry-bo-dy here, good-bye, so long, fare-well.
3. Good-bye, so long, fare-well, my friends, good-bye, so long, fare-well. We'll see you soon a-gain, and then we'll make Mu-sic To-ge-ther a-gain.

Slower

And how 'bout a hug for your mom or dad, or the one who takes care of you? And a hug or a hand-shake for your friends, and then how 'bout one just for your-self, too?

When it's time to say goodbye to children or friends, try singing this song. It's a good reminder that you'll see each other again soon!

Sing the name of your child, holding younger ones and swaying to the waltz beat. You can also evoke the feeling of the song by just humming it or singing it on "la" or "doo." When you and your child must separate for a time, this song may be very helpful. Sing it before you leave the room, returning with the "Hello Song." Or try it while walking your child to the preschool door. The rhythm and tempo of the song make it especially appealing—walking could turn into skipping or dancing!

Recording: Piano, bass, shaker, triangle

MUSICAL MEMORIES

MUSICAL MEMORIES

GLOSSARY

Audiation. "Hearing" music when it is not physically present—the mental process allowing a person to "think" music and create it.

Basic music competence. The ability to sing in tune and move with accurate rhythm. While many children in our culture can develop this inborn potential by the age of five or six, kindergarteners with little music experience often cannot sing in tune or move to a beat. With a sufficiently rich music environment, however, a child can do so as early as age three or four.

Beat. Music's basic pulse. The main beat that most people would naturally tap to a song. We call this consensus beat the *macrobeat*.

Downbeat. The first, slightly stronger beat in a music measure.

Drone. A tone or pitch, usually a resting tone or related note, that is sustained or repeated throughout a long section of music, regardless of the shifting harmonic relationships that may occur.

Harmony. Two or more notes sounding together, thus creating a pleasing or interesting sound.

Macrobeat. What most listeners would agree is the basic pulse of a song. It is the main,"big" beat, in contrast to the smaller *microbeat*.

Measure. A group of macrobeats (usually from two to four) with the first beat slightly accented. In music notation, each measure is enclosed by vertical lines called bar lines.

Meter. Beats are usually grouped in recurring pulses of twos or threes, creating what we call either duple meter (like a march) or triple meter (like a waltz), with the first note of each group slightly accented. Some songs have a pulse which combines groups of two *and* three beats within a single phrase, resulting in an asymmetrical or "unusual" meter.

Microbeat. The first subdivision of the macrobeat or basic pulse of the music. This "small" beat is faster: two macrobeats per measure (duple meter) would become four microbeats when subdivided, while three macrobeats per measure (triple meter) would be subdivided into six microbeats.

Music achievement. What we are able to do with our natural aptitude for music. This includes singing in tune in and moving with accurate rhythm, as well as learning to play an instrument, making up melodies, or improvising musically with friends and family.

Music aptitude. The inborn potential for music learning and growth. While this is determined biologically, as far as we know, it can also be influenced by the surrounding environment. Before the age of five, music aptitude is especially malleable: rich and varied music experience can help it develop, while lack of experience leads to atrophy. By the age of nine, as neurological pathways in the brain begin to mature, the child's music aptitude stabilizes.

Offbeats. Rather than accenting the downbeat (see above), certain types of music accent offbeats or "backbeats" for musical effect. For example, gospel music often emphasizes clapping on beats 2 and 4.

Ostinato. A short musical phrase or pattern which can be repeated over and over again to accompany the rest of the song.

Play. The delightful way by which young children teach themselves: they observe, imitate, explore, experiment, practice, and create.

Primary music development. The period in a child's life when his developing brain is most open to musical influence and growth. During this time, the child moves through predictable, observable stages of music learning culminating in *basic music competence*. Exposure to a variety of music and movement experiences is crucial during this period, when the child learns so fast and so well.

Resting tone. The tonal note in a song where the music comes to "rest," usually the last note of the song. This note is also called "do," "1," and the "tonic."

Resting tone chord. The basic chord derived from a song, which includes the resting tone and the third and fifth notes above it. Sounding together, these three notes form a "chord" which most people find pleasing. Very young children often sound the resting tone or the fifth note spontaneously after hearing a song, an important first step in achieving tonal competence. This chord is also called the "tonic" or "1" chord.

Rhythm patterns. Short rhythmic phrases, generally based upon and directly following a song or chant in a Music Together class or recording. These patterns intentionally have no melodic component, in order to provide an experience of only the rhythmic aspect of music. Children learn by imitating these basic building blocks of rhythm and by making up some of their own.

Round. A song which goes "around" again. One voice (or group of voices) begins singing the melody followed by two to four other voices (or groups) singing the same melody but beginning at successively later times. The melody of the round is cleverly designed to "fit" harmonically, despite being out of phase with itself several times over.

S.Q. or Silly Quotient. A Music Together takeoff on I.Q. (intelligence quotient). Young children are very serious about being silly. It helps drive their interest in play, one of their primary learning strategies. Children respect authentic S.Q. in the adults around them, and a genuine grasp of it can increase a teacher's effectiveness in the classroom. It also creates more fun for everyone!

Tonal patterns. Groups of two or three notes, based upon and following a song just sung in a Music Together class or recording. The tones intentionally have no rhythmic component, in order to provide an experience of only the tonal aspect of music. Imitating and playing with tonal patterns can help children organize their musical thought so they can sing and create songs.

Vocables. Vocal sounds or syllables, such as "bom," "doo," or "la." When sung in melodies, they carry no semantic meaning but are integrated in sound and rhythm into the music.

GUITAR REFERENCE CHART

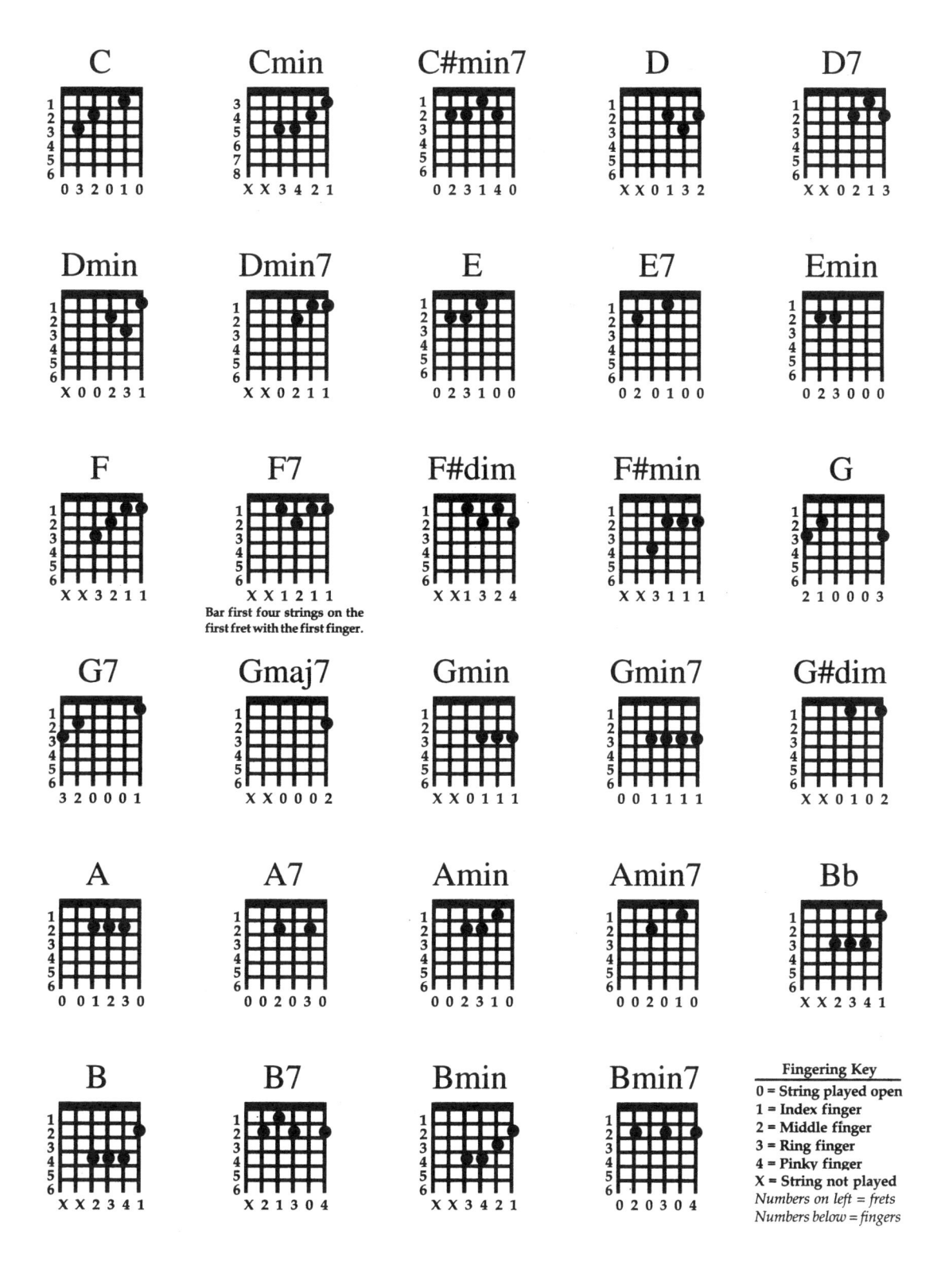

Bar first four strings on the first fret with the first finger. (under F)

Fingering Key
- 0 = String played open
- 1 = Index finger
- 2 = Middle finger
- 3 = Ring finger
- 4 = Pinky finger
- X = String not played
- *Numbers on left = frets*
- *Numbers below = fingers*

REFERENCES

Gardner, Howard. *Multiple Intelligences: The Theory in Practice*. New York: BasicBooks, 1993.

Gordon, Edwin E. *A Music Learning Theory for Newborn and Young Children*. Chicago: GIA Publication, Inc., 1997.

Guilmartin, Kenneth K., and Lili M. Levinowitz. *Music and Your Child: A Guide for Parents and Caregivers*. Princeton, NJ: Center for Music and Young Children, 1989.

Holt, John. *How Children Learn*. New York: Dell Publishing Co., Inc., 1983.

Machover, Wilma, and Marienne Uszler. *Sound Choices: Guiding Your Child's Musical Experiences*. New York: Oxford University Press, Inc., 1996.

Pearce, Joseph Chilton. *Evolution's End: Claiming the Potential of Our Intelligence*. San Francisco: HarperSanFrancisco, 1992.

Pearce, Joseph Chilton. *Magical Child*. New York: Bantam Books, Inc., 1980.

ACKNOWLEDGMENTS

The authors would like to acknowledge the major sources of influence on the ongoing evolution of Music Together since it first began to take shape in the mid-eighties. The work of Emile Jaques-Dalcroze, particularly as interpreted by Robert M. Abramson, is fundamental to Ken Guilmartin's approach to music and movement education. Lili Levinowitz became inspired by the music learning theory of Edwin F. Gordon and worked with him closely as Director of the Children's Music Development program at Temple University, where she obtained her Ph.D. Both authors wish to acknowledge the ongoing research and creative field applications of their colleagues, and they are especially grateful for the feedback and inspirational enthusiasm of Music Together teachers, center directors, and families everywhere.

To create a truly developmentally appropriate program, the authors looked beyond music education to the field of early childhood education. Especially notable among many influences is Ken's eight-year experience with the Montclair Cooperative School as a parent and faculty member, and for both authors, the inspiration of parenting their own children, Eli Levinowitz and Lauren Guilmartin.

Finally, both authors wish to thank David K. Sengstack who provided both the initial vision and the means to begin this wonderful work.

TAMBOURINE Production Team—

Lyn Ransom, program development
Catherine Judd Hirsch, production editing
Susan Pujdak Hoffman, additional writing and editing
Marcel Chouteau, Jennifer Leach, Julie Sansone, production assistance
Music Together editorial review committee: Susan Darrow, Deanna deCampos, Susan Hoffman, Jackie Jacobs, Sally Woodson
Robert Bowen, music engraving
Main Street Design, logos and songbook design
Janet Payne, illustrations

Please feel free to contact us!
www.musictogether.com
(800) 728-2692
For Music Together parent-child class locations: x306
For CDs, songbooks, or child-friendly instruments: x345
For teacher training and workshops: x322

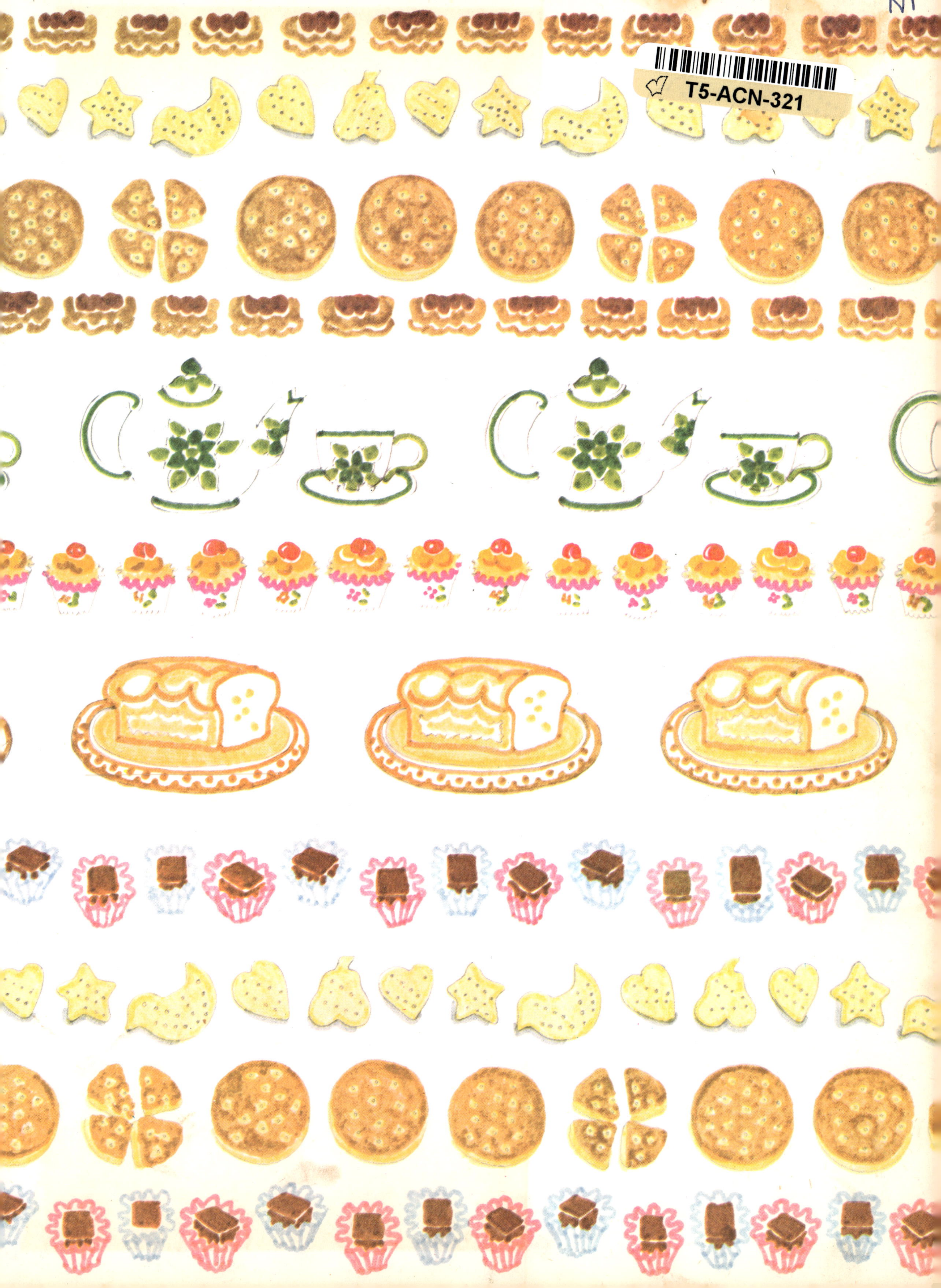

COOKING IS EASY
when you know how

ARCO PUBLISHING COMPANY, INC.
New York

Author
Isabelle Barrett

Illustrations
Joy Simpson

Photographs
Alan Duns
Front cover—Roger Phillips

Typography and Design
Brian Liddle

Editor
Karen Harriman

Published by Arco Publishing Company, Inc.
219 Park Avenue South, New York, N.Y. 10003

Copyright © 1974 by Marshall Cavendish Publications Limited

All rights reserved

Library of Congress Catalog Card Number 74-76264

ISBN 0-668-03481-5

Printed in Great Britain

This edition not to be sold outside the U.S.A. or Canada

About This Book

Cooking is fun—and it's creative too! We hope that with this cookery book you'll have a great time experimenting and that you'll dazzle your parents—as well as your friends—with all the good things that you'll turn out.

All the recipes are easy so that you can cook them yourself (with perhaps a little help from your mother). You'll find quick snacks, after school treats, a Sunday lunch dish, delicious cakes, super desserts and even a recipe for bread!

Be sure to read the next few pages before you start cooking—they'll explain some basic cookery terms and techniques that you should know and they'll help your mother, too.

So good luck—and remember that the important thing is to make good things to eat and to enjoy doing it!

Contents

Pancakes	6-7
Scotch Broth	8-9
Baked Alaska	10-11
Sausage Rolls	12-13
Hamburgers	14-15
Strawberry Trifle	16-17
Chocolate Fudge Sauce	18-19
Eggs in a Nest	20-21
Brownies	22-23
Witches' Froth	24-25
Surprise Packets	26-28
Butterscotch Bananas	29
Creamy Orange Snow Tart	30-31
Meat Pasties	32-33
Bread	34-35
Queen of Puddings	36-37
Shortbread	38-39
Liver, Bacon and Apple Hot Pot	40-41
Chocolate Fudge	42-43
Fairy Cakes	44-45
Mince Pies	46-47
Toad in the Hole	48

There are some basic things which every cook should know about which we thought we'd put at the beginning of the book so that you'd read them first and be prepared before you start cooking.

★ Clean hands and fingers make food tastier too—so make sure you wash yours thoroughly before you start.

★ Always wear an apron when you cook—that way you'll keep your clothes clean and you can be as messy as you like to be when you're cooking.

★ Always use proper oven gloves when you're putting things into the oven and taking them out again. Or ask your mother to do this for you.

★ Be sure to read the recipe all the way through before you begin cooking.

★ It will make things easier if you put out and weigh all your ingredients before you start cooking.

★ Don't use any sharp knives; if you have any chopping to do ask your mother to help you.

★ Do be careful when you turn the stove on and off and when you're raising or reducing heat.

★ It's a good idea to turn pot handles to the side of the stove. This can prevent lots of nasty accidents.

★ The best cooks always wash up their dirty dishes as they go along and even if you don't do that the first time you try a recipe, do try to do it as you become more expert in the kitchen—there's nothing more off-putting than having to tackle a huge washing-up just after you've popped the cake in the oven and are thinking of going off to play for a bit while it cooks!

WEIGHTS and MEASURES

You should try to be as accurate as possible in weighing and measuring ingredients. Hopefully your mother has kitchen scales and measuring cups and spoons if you're European or British, measuring cups and spoons if you're American or Canadian. In both cases, it's fun—and a challenge—to use them. We often ask you to roll out dough to measurements such as 6 cm ($\frac{1}{4}$ in). These are only approximate thicknesses and if you don't have a ruler handy, don't despair.

Note Because we're hoping that boys and girls of many nationalities will read this book and try out the recipes, we have had to make allowances for the different measuring customs in different countries. In Britain, for instance, good cooks will soon be measuring everything in metric measurements but in the United States ingredients are measured in special measuring spoons and cups. We have indicated these methods by putting the metric measurement first followed by the American measurement in square brackets—[ ]. So the ingredients are listed like this:

25 g [2 tablespoons] butter
25 g [$\frac{1}{4}$ cup] flour

For mothers who may not be familiar with the metric measures, the chart below may be useful in converting ounces into grammes, fluid ounces into millilitres, and inches into centimetres. The recommended equivalents shown are not always exact, but have been rounded off for ease of conversion.

Chart

Ounces	Grammes	Fluid Ounces	Millilitres
1	25	1	28.4
2	50	5	142
3	75	10	284
4	100	15	426
5	125	20 (1 pint)	568 ($\frac{1}{2}$ litre)
6	150		
7	175		
8	200		
16 (1 lb)	400		

Inches	Centimetres	Inches	Centimetres
$\frac{1}{4}$	0.6	2	5
$\frac{1}{2}$	1.3	3	7.5
$\frac{3}{4}$	2	4	10
1	2.5	5	12.5

Here are some general and handy-hints to make things easier for you as you start.

Eggs

Eggs are used a lot in cooking, as you will see when you start to read the recipes. Usually all that you need to do is crack the shells so that the insides come out, but sometimes you'll need to know a bit more. So we thought we'd tell you some basic things about eggs.

How to Break Open an Egg

Hold the egg over a bowl (or in the case of Eggs in a Nest—over a frying-pan) and gently crack the shell against the side.

Using both hands, gently pull the shell apart at the crack.

The egg white and yolk should fall out quite easily as the crack widens.

How to Separate an Egg

Have two bowls ready, standing side by side.

Crack open the egg. Let the white run into the bowl you've used to crack the egg against. While the white is running out, carefully tip the yolk from one egg shell half to the other. When all the white is in the bowl, put the yolk in the second bowl.

How to Beat Egg Whites

Place a medium-sized bowl on a flat surface and have a wire whisk or a rotary beater ready.

Crack open and separate the egg whites and yolks. Make sure there's no egg yolk in with the whites and if there is a little, scoop it out with a bit of the shell.

Using the whisk or beater, beat the whites very hard for a long time so that they will stand up in peaks if you lift the whisk or beater out of the bowl.

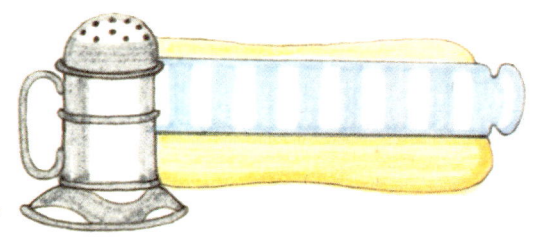

Pastry

We've used pastry quite a lot in this book and, on the whole, we've suggested that you use frozen pre-made pastry dough because it's much easier than making your own (and don't be ashamed—lots of adults, including us, use it a lot of the time, too!). But there are one or two little tips you should know before you start to use pastry or make batter.

Pastry dough gets best results when it is very cold (straight from the refrigerator) but thawed out, of course, if it's frozen pastry.

ALWAYS use a large flat surface to roll out pastry dough—if your mother doesn't have a large pastry board, use the kitchen table or the top of a large kitchen cupboard. Anyway, you'll need lots of elbow room.

AND ALWAYS remember to sprinkle flour over the pastry board or surface AND the rolling pin before you start to roll out dough—otherwise it might stick.

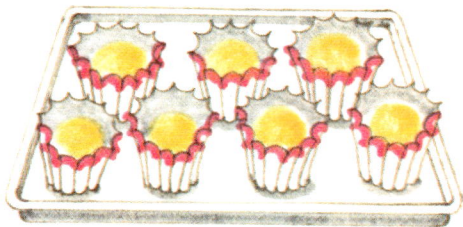

Baking

Batter (for fairy cakes, for instance) is easier to make if all the ingredients you use are warmed to room temperature—butter especially is much easier to beat if it's soft.

Baking sheets and tins should sometimes be greased before you use them—and we have told you when this is necessary in a recipe. To grease a baking sheet or tin, place the measured amount of butter or oil on a folded kitchen paper towel. Rub it all over the inside surfaces of the sheet or tin—especially into the corners.

Bread

We've given you one bread recipe in this book. Making bread is one of the most satisfying things a cook can bake—and if you follow the recipe carefully, you'll be able to present a super loaf to your parents (much nicer than one bought in the shops). To make bread, you need to know a few important points:

You are using yeast which is a living substance that makes your flour mixture grow. We have suggested dried yeast (the plants are inert and will not become active until they are mixed with a warm liquid), but whether you use fresh or dried yeast, remember that yeast is destroyed by extreme heat. So don't use hot water and don't leave the dough to rise in a very hot place.

Kneading the dough is fun and it is done to mix the flour thoroughly with the liquid. Turn the dough out on to a lightly floured surface. Fold it over on to itself towards you and then press it down away from you with the heels of your hands. Turn the dough slightly and fold and press again. Continue kneading for about 10 minutes—by then the dough should feel smooth and elastic.

The dough should be left to rise in a warm draught-free place—and can't be hurried—until it has almost doubled in bulk. To test if it has risen enough, press two clean fingers deep into the dough and take them out quickly. If the indentation remains the rising is completed.

Pancakes

Pancakes are so much fun to make. This recipe is a basic one and can be filled with savoury fillings such as chopped cooked meat or vegetables. If you would rather have sweet pancakes —so that you can fill them to overflowing with jam or honey or mashed bananas—add 1 tablespoon of sugar to the basic flour and milk batter. We've only estimated the number of the pancakes because the number made will depend on the size of the frying-pan you're using.

You Will Need
for 4 people

100 g [1 cup] flour
$\frac{1}{8}$ teaspoon salt
2 eggs
25 g [2 tablespoons] melted butter
115 ml [$\frac{1}{2}$ cup] milk
85 ml [$\frac{3}{8}$ cup] water
2 tablespoons vegetable oil

1 Sift the flour and the salt into a medium-sized mixing bowl. (This is to make sure there are no lumps in the flour.)

2 Make a hollow in the middle of the flour mixture. Crack open the eggs and drop them both into the hollow. Then pour in the melted butter.

3 Gradually add the milk and the water, beating the mixture with a wooden spoon. Continue beating until there are no lumps left.

4 Cover the bowl with a clean cloth and set it aside for 30 minutes. You could start preparing some scrumptious fillings to put inside the pancakes while you're waiting.

5 Uncover the bowl. With a pastry brush lightly grease a heavy frying-pan with a little of the vegetable oil. (Just dip the brush in the oil — it will retain enough to grease the pan.)

6 Place the frying-pan over moderate heat and warm the pan (and that little bit of oil) until it is very hot.

7 Remove the frying-pan from the heat and pour about 4 tablespoons of the batter into the centre of the pan.

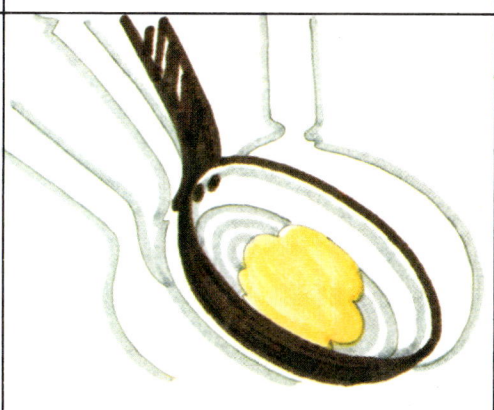

8 Quickly tilt the pan in all directions until there is a thin layer of batter all over it. Return the pan to the heat.

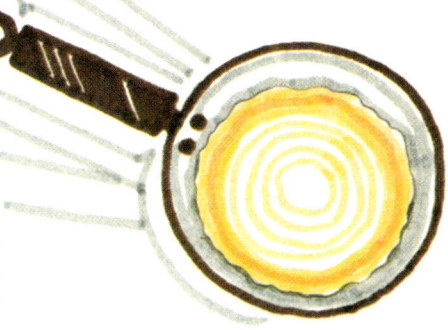

9 Cook the pancake for 1 minute. Shake the pan gently to loosen the pancake. To see if it is cooked, lift one edge with a fish slice or spatula. It should be a light golden colour all over.

10 With the fish slice or spatula, carefully turn the pancake by lifting it up and over. You could toss it but do be careful!

11 Cook the second side for 30 seconds. (This side will be less evenly browned than the first one and is the side on which you should spread your filling.)

12 Slide the pancake from the pan on to a warmed plate. Cook the remaining batter in the same way, greasing the pan each time. Stuff and roll the pancakes while they are warm.

Scotch Broth

Here's a super soup—so full of good things, it's a meal in itself. You should start to make it at least 3 hours before you want to eat it.

You Will Need
for 4 people

1 l [5 cups] hot water

1 beef stock cube

400 g [1 lb] neck of lamb (ask the butcher to cut it into pieces and to cut off any fat)

2 tablespoons pearl barley

½ teaspoon salt

½ teaspoon pepper

½ teaspoon dried thyme

⅛ teaspoon cayenne pepper

2 carrots

1 turnip

2 leeks

1 Pour the hot water into a very large jug and add the stock cube. Stir briskly with a fork or spoon until the cube has dissolved.

2 Put the lamb pieces and the barley into a very large saucepan and pour in the beef stock. Add the salt, pepper, thyme and cayenne.

3 Place the pan over high heat and bring the mixture to the boil. Turn the heat down to low and simmer the broth for 2 hours.

4 Cut off the ends from the carrots, turnip and leeks. Using a knife, scrape the carrots and peel the turnip. Pull off the outer leaves of the leeks.

5 Wash all the vegetables very thoroughly under cold running water.

6 Using the knife, chop all of the vegetables into small pieces.

11 The broth is now ready to serve. You could either pour it into a large, warmed soup tureen or into individual soup bowls. Serve at once, while it is still hot.

10 Using a knife, remove the meat from the bones. It should come away from the bones very easily. Cut the meat into small pieces, then return it to the broth. Throw away the bones.

When the broth has simmered for hours, put the chopped vegetables into it. (Vegetables don't need to cook nearly as long as meat, that's why they're added later.)

8 Continue to simmer the broth for a further hour.

9 When the broth has simmered for 1 hour, using a slotted spoon, lift the meat out of the broth and put it on a chopping board or very large plate.

Baked Alaska

It's not often you put ice-cream in the oven to 'bake', but for Baked Alaska you do. The result is unbelievably good—as you'll see when you bite into this fantastic meringue and ice-cream mixture.

You Will Need
for 4 people

568 ml [1 pint] ice-cream block (vanilla is probably best for this recipe but use your particular favourite, if you'd prefer)

1 large sponge cake (if you can buy a square one, that would be best)

6 tablespoons apricot or raspberry jam (or any thick jam will do)

4 eggs

⅛ teaspoon salt

50 g [¼ cup] castor sugar

Before you begin, turn on the oven to very high 450°F (Gas Mark 8, 230°C).

Keep the ice-cream in the freezing compartment of the refrigerator until just before you need it.

1 Put the sponge cake on a chopping board and, using a knife, trim it so that it is the same size and shape as the block of ice-cream.

2 Transfer the sponge cake to a baking sheet and spread the jam all over the top, as evenly as you can. Set the cake aside.

3 Separate the egg whites from the yolks. (For how to separate eggs, see page 5). Make sure there's no egg yolk in the egg whites. If any falls in scoop it out. Keep the egg yolks for other recipes.

4 Add the salt to the egg whites and, using a wire whisk or rotary beater, beat the whites briskly until they are frothy. (For how to do this, see page 5.)

5 Gradually add the sugar, beating constantly until the egg whites are very stiff.

6 Now, very quickly, take the ice-cream out of the refrigerator and unwrap it. Place the ice-cream on top of the jam on the sponge cake.

7 With a spatula, cover the ice-cream and cake with the egg whites. Make sure the ice-cream and cake are completely covered or the ice-cream will melt in the oven.

8 Put the baking sheet in the centre of the oven and leave to bake for ONLY 3 minutes.

9 The meringue should be a very light golden colour. If it is cooked, it should be removed from the oven.

10 Eat Baked Alaska the MINUTE it comes out of the oven!

11

Sausage Rolls

Eaten hot or cold as after-school treats, these sausage rolls will satisfy your hunger. And they're fun to make.

You Will Need
for about 12 sausage rolls

300 g [3 cups] frozen puff pastry dough (don't forget to thaw it out before you use it, though!)

1 egg

400 g [1 lb] sausages (thin ones, called chipolata are best, but you can buy big ones and cut them in half, lengthways)

Before you begin, turn on the oven to hot 425°F (Gas Mark 7, 220°C).

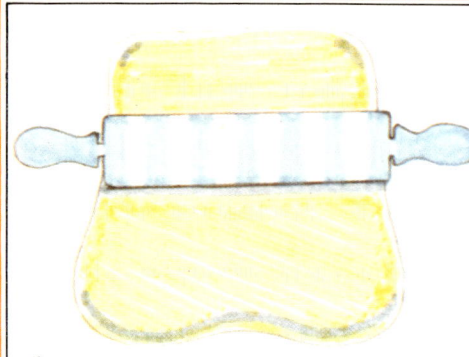

1 On a pastry board that has been sprinkled with a little flour, roll out the dough to about 6 cm [¼-inch] thick (it should be about 30.5 cm [12-inches] square).

2 Using a knife dipped in hot water, cut the dough into 3 strips, each about 10 cm [4-inches] wide.

3 Now cut each strip into 4 pieces. Each piece of dough should be about 7.5 cm [3-inches] by 10 cm [4-inches].

12

4 Break the egg into a cup (for how to do this, see page 5). Beat the egg thoroughly with a fork and set it aside.

5 Lay a sausage, or a half sausage, near one edge of each piece of dough.

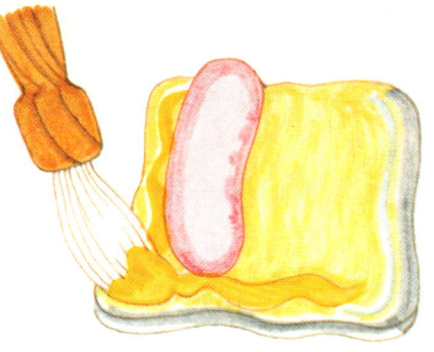

6 With a pastry brush, or a finger (a clean one though!), brush a little of the beaten egg along all the edges of the dough.

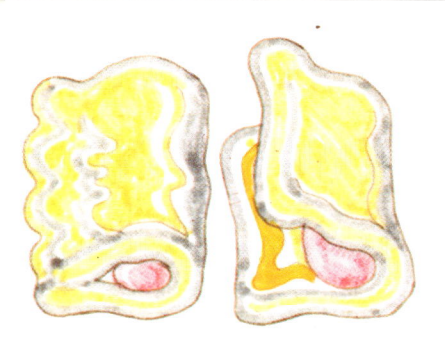

7 Fold the dough over the top of the sausage, or half sausage, and press the two edges together: the egg will seal them together.

8 Put all the rolls on a baking sheet, with about 2.5 cm [1-inch] of space between each roll.

9 With a knife, make a hole in each roll so that the steam can escape while the rolls are baking. Brush more of the beaten egg on top so that the pastry will be golden when cooked.

10 Place the baking sheet in the oven and bake the rolls for 20 minutes.

11 If the pastry is not golden and crisp at this point, bake the rolls for a few minutes longer. Remove from the oven.

12 Serve the rolls hot or cold—perhaps with mustard or pickles.

13

Hamburgers

Hamburgers are, of course, a traditional—and favourite—American dish and once you've tasted this version you'll know exactly why! Serve Hamburgers with a variety of relishes and and some fizzy cola drinks. Don't forget that hamburgers should be eaten with your hands.

You Will Need
for 4 people

4 hamburger buns
2 thick slices white bread
800 g lean minced beef [2 lb ground beef]
$\frac{1}{4}$ teaspoon salt
$\frac{1}{2}$ teaspoon pepper
$\frac{1}{2}$ teaspoon dried thyme
1 small egg

Before you begin, turn on the grill [broiler] to high.

1 Split open the buns and place them on the grill [broiler] rack. Toast the bun halves until they are browned. Remove them from the heat and set aside. Leave the grill [broiler] on.

2 On a chopping board, cut off and throw away the crusts from the bread. Then, using your hands, tear the bread into very small pieces.

3 Put the minced [ground] beef, the torn-up bread pieces, salt, pepper, thyme and the egg into a large mixing bowl. Squeeze them together with your hands until they are well mixed.

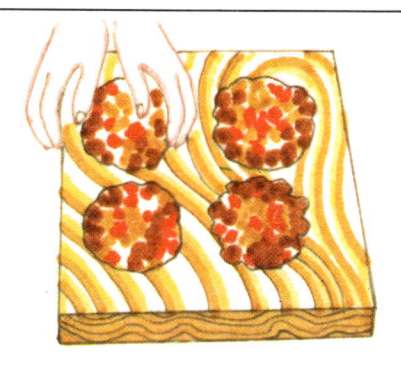

4 Turn the mixture out on to a chopping board and, again using your hands, form the beef mixture into 4 equal-sized balls.

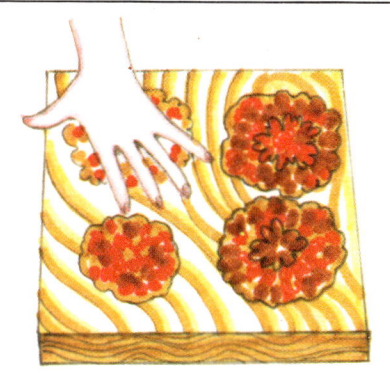

5 Using the palm of your hand, flatten the beef balls into flat patties, about 2 cm [¾-inch] thick.

6 Place the 4 beef patties on the grill [broiler] rack and put them under the grill [broiler].

7 Grill [broil] them for 3 minutes on each side or until the hamburgers are evenly browned. Turn the hamburgers over with a fish slice or spatula.

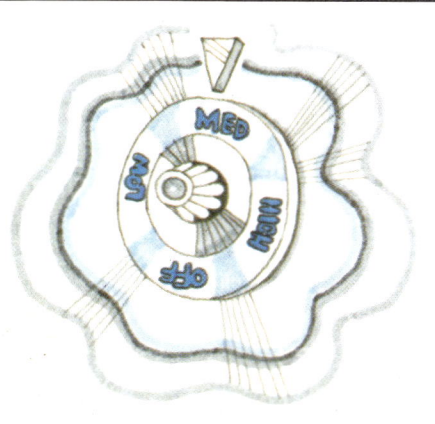

8 Reduce the grill [broiler] heat to moderate.

9 Grill [broil] the hamburgers for a further 7 minutes on each side or until they are cooked through. (They should be only very faintly pink on the inside.)

When the hamburgers are cooked, remove them from the grill [broiler]. Place 1 hamburger on each of the 4 bottom halves of the buns. Place the top half on top of the hamburgers. Hamburgers are usually served with a selection of relishes and tomato ketchup, mayonnaise and mustard.

Strawberry Trifle

You Will Need
for 4 people

1 packet strawberry jelly [gelatin]

12 small stale sponge cakes, thickly sliced

4 tablespoons strawberry jam

200 g [8 oz] canned strawberries

25 g [3 tablespoons] custard powder

2 tablespoons sugar

568 ml [2½ cups] milk

142 ml double cream [⅝ cup heavy cream]

Trifle is one of the very nicest desserts ever invented—and this is an especially good version! If you prefer raspberries or blackberries, use them instead of the strawberries.

1 Make up the jelly [gelatin] following the instructions on the packet. Set it aside.

2 Put the sponge cake slices on the bottom of a large glass bowl. (Cut them to fit if necessary.) Then spread over the jam.

3 Pour the syrup from the canned strawberries over the sponge cake mixture and set the dish aside for 5 minutes so that the cakes can soak up the liquid. Set the strawberries aside.

7 When the milk is just beginning to bubble, quickly remove the pan from the heat and pour the milk on to the custard mixture, stirring constantly to prevent any lumps from forming.

8 Pour the custard back into the pan and return the pan to low heat. Cook, stirring with a wooden spoon, for 2 minutes or until the custard boils. Remove from the heat and set aside.

9 When the custard is cool, pour it over the mixture in the glass bowl. Set it aside.

4 When the jelly [gelatin] is just beginning to set, pour it over the sponge cake mixture. Set aside.

5 Meanwhile, in a large mixing bowl, mix the custard powder and the sugar together. Stir in 3 tablespoons of the milk and beat well until the ingredients form a smooth paste.

6 Pour the rest of the milk into a saucepan and put the pan over low heat. (Keep watching the milk while it heats—don't let it boil over.)

10 In a medium-sized bowl, beat the cream with a wire whisk or rotary beater until it is very thick.

11 Pour or spoon the cream over the custard.

12 Decorate the top with the reserved strawberries and serve.

17

Chocolate Fudge Sauce

Serve this delicious Chocolate Fudge Sauce hot or cold spooned over your favourite ice-cream.

You Will Need
for 110 ml [½ cup] sauce

- 50 g dark (2 squares semi-sweet) cooking chocolate, broken into small pieces
- 100 g [½ cup] butter
- 2 tablespoons golden [light corn] syrup
- 57 ml [¼ cup] boiling water
- 150 g [¾ cup] castor sugar
- 1 teaspoon vanilla essence

1 Put the chocolate pieces and all the remaining ingredients into a medium-sized heatproof bowl.

2 Half-fill a large saucepan with hot water and place the bowl in it.

3 Place the saucepan with the bowl in it over very low heat and cook, stirring constantly with a wooden spoon, until the mixture is smooth and the ingredients are well blended.

4 Increase the heat to moderate and cook the mixture, stirring frequently, until it comes to the boil.

5 Boil the mixture for 3 minutes. Remove the pan from the heat.

6 If you are serving the sauce cold, allow it to cool to room temperature. Then place the bowl in the refrigerator to chill for 1 hour or until the sauce is really cold.

If you are serving the sauce hot, pour it over ice-cream or fruit and serve at once.

19

Eggs in a nest

This is a marvellous dish to serve at any time of the day—for instance, try it for a filling Sunday breakfast or 'brunch' or for supper.

You Will Need
for 4 people

4 slices streaky bacon

500 g [20 oz] canned baked beans

4 eggs

4 slices toasted bread

1 Using a knife, cut the bacon slices into small pieces.

2 Put the bacon pieces into a medium-sized frying-pan and place the pan over moderate heat.

3 Fry the bacon quite gently, stirring frequently, for 5 minutes or until it is brown and crisp.

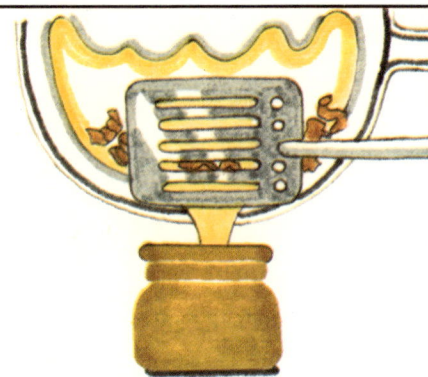

4 Carefully pour off the bacon fat from the pan into a heatproof bowl. (Keep it nearby because it will be used later on in the recipe.)

5 Add the baked beans to the bacon pieces in the frying-pan and stir to mix well. Cook the beans and bacon, stirring occasionally, for 5 minutes.

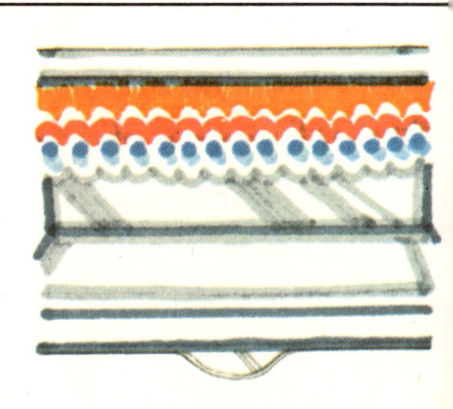

6 Turn on the grill [broiler] to high and leave it to heat up.

20

7 Using a tablespoon, make 4 hollows in the beans mixture in the frying-pan.

8 Break 1 egg open and drop it into one of the hollows. (For how to do this see page 5.) Do the same thing with the other eggs, so that all 4 hollows are filled.

9 Cover the pan with a lid and cook the mixture for 2 minutes.

10 Remove the lid from the pan and spoon the reserved bacon fat over the eggs.

11 Remove the frying-pan from the heat and put it under the grill [broiler]. Grill [broil] the mixture until the eggs have set.

12 Remove the pan from under the grill [broiler] and carefully transfer the mixture to a warmed serving dish or to individual serving plates. Serve with the toast slices.

21

Brownies

Brownies aren't just junior Girl Guides or Girl Scouts—in the United States, they are a type of delicious chocolate nut square. They just demand to be eaten—especially with a glass of cold milk.

You Will Need

for about 16 brownies

1 teaspoon butter

150 g dark [6 squares semi-sweet] cooking chocolate, broken into small pieces

2 tablespoons cold water

100 g [½ cup] butter

100 g [½ cup] castor sugar

1 teaspoon vanilla essence

100 g [1 cup] self-raising flour

2 eggs

50 g [⅓ cup] walnuts, chopped into small pieces

Before you begin, turn on the oven to warm 325°F (Gas Mark 3, 170°C).

1 Using the teaspoon of butter, lightly grease a 20.5 cm [8-inch] square baking tin.

2 Put the chocolate pieces, water and butter into a medium-sized saucepan.

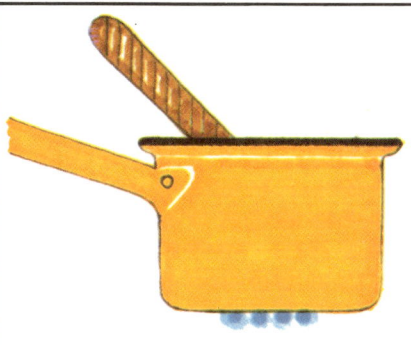

3 Place the pan over very low heat and cook the mixture, stirring occasionally with a wooden spoon, until the chocolate and butter have melted and the mixture is smooth.

4 Remove the pan from the heat and stir in the castor sugar and vanilla essence. Beat the mixture until the sugar has dissolved and all the ingredients are well mixed.

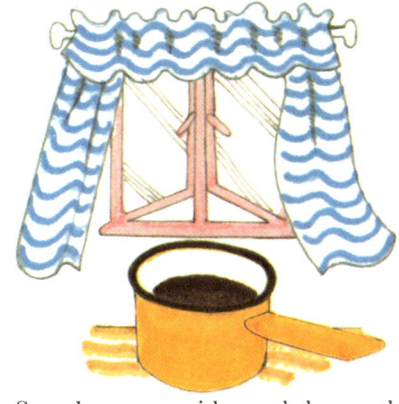

5 Set the pan aside and leave the mixture until it is cool. (This will take about 15 minutes.)

6 Sift the flour into a medium-sized bowl. (This is to make sure there are no lumps in the flour.) Gradually add the cooled chocolate mixture to the flour, stirring constantly.

7 Then add the eggs and beat well until the mixture is quite smooth. Add the walnut pieces and stir them well into the mixture.

8 Pour the mixture into the prepared baking tin. Put the tin in the oven and bake for 35 minutes.

9 The brownies should be cooked—to test if they are, insert a knife into the centre. The knife will come out clean if the brownies are cooked.

10 Remove the tin from the oven and set it aside to cool for about 30 minutes. When the mixture is cool, cut it into squares and eat!

Witches Froth

The good white witches invented this one—a frothy banana dessert topped with yummy chocolate—so why not make it for a Halloween party?

You Will Need
for 4 people

- 6 bananas, peeled
- 3 tablespoons lemon juice
- 284 ml [1¼ cups] fruit yogurt
- 4 tablespoons castor sugar
- 2 egg whites
- 142 ml double cream [⅝ cup heavy cream]
- 50 g [2 oz] eating chocolate

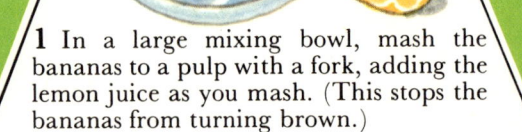

1 In a large mixing bowl, mash the bananas to a pulp with a fork, adding the lemon juice as you mash. (This stops the bananas from turning brown.)

2 Stir the yogurt and castor sugar into the bananas and beat with the fork until they are well mixed.

3 In a medium-sized mixing bowl, beat the egg whites with a wire whisk or a rotary beater until they are stiff. (For how to do this see page 5.)

4 In another medium-sized mixing bowl, beat the cream with a wire whisk or rotary beater until it is thick.

5 Using a metal spoon, gently stir a spoonful of cream into the banana mixture, then a spoonful of egg whites.

6 Continue doing this until all the cream and egg whites have been added and the ingredients are well mixed.

7 Pile the froth into a pretty serving dish.

8 Place the dish in the refrigerator and leave the mixture to chill for 30 minutes.

9 Grate the chocolate on the fine side of a grater.

10 Remove the banana froth from the refrigerator and sprinkle over the chocolate gratings.

If you're serving the froth on Halloween, why not decorate it with this witches' hat? To make it, cut out the two shapes, as shown on the picture, from black paper. Curl the quarter-circle round to make a cone, bend the tabs up and push the brim down over the cone.

25

Surprise Packets

Lots of food can be cooked over a fire (or in an oven) wrapped up in little parcels —using aluminium foil.

Did you know you can barbecue corn in aluminium foil? Just remove the husk and silky strands, rub the corn with softened butter and salt and pepper. Wrap it in a double thickness of foil, twist and fold the ends to seal and cook it for 15 to 20 minutes, depending on the heat of the fire. Or what about barbecued bananas? Choose 4 firm bananas, place them on a barbecue and cook them until the skins turn black. Turn them occasionally with tongs. Remove the bananas carefully from the fire with the tongs. Carefully peel back the top layer of the skin. Serve them with whipped cream.

You Will Need
for 4 people

4 large chicken legs

1 teaspoon salt

1 teaspoon pepper

1 teaspoon dried rosemary

1 large onion

25 g [2 tablespoons] butter, cut into small pieces

4 large potatoes

25 g [2 tablespoons] very soft butter

1 Sprinkle the chicken legs with the salt and pepper then rub it into the skin. Sprinkle the rosemary over the chicken legs.

2 Cut out 4 squares of aluminium foil, each large enough to enclose 1 chicken leg. Place a chicken leg in the centre of each square. Set aside.

3 Cut off the ends from the onion and peel off its outer skin with a knife. Place the onion on a chopping board and slice crosswise, so that you have lots of onion rings.

4 Divide the rings equally among the chicken placing them on top of the meat. Then dot the small butter pieces on top and fold over the foil so that the chicken is enclosed.

5 Place the parcels on the oven shelf over the barbecue fire and cook them, turning them over once or twice, for 5 minutes.

6 Move the parcels to the edge of the shelf over the fire and leave them there turning them over once or twice for 45 minutes.

7 Meanwhile, scrub all the dirt off the potatoes. Prick them all over with a fork so that later when they are cooking the hot steam can escape.

8 Cut out 4 squares of foil, each large enough to enclose 1 potato. Smear each piece of foil with ¼ of the very soft butter. Place a potato in the centre of each square and fold as before.

9 Put the potatoes on the shelf above the barbecue fire and cook them, turning them once or twice, for 45 minutes.

10 When the chicken and potatoes are both cooked, remove them from the fire and serve them hot.

Butterscotch Bananas

You can eat this delicious dish either hot or cold—and if you would rather have it cold, then serve it with your favourite ice-cream for a special treat.

You Will Need
for 4 people

4 bananas

8 teaspoons soft brown sugar

25 g [2 tablespoons] butter

Before you begin turn on the grill [broiler] to high.

1 Peel the bananas, then, using a knife, cut them in half, lengthways. Put them in a flameproof baking dish and set it aside.

2 Put the sugar and the butter into a small saucepan.

3 Place the saucepan over low heat and cook the mixture, stirring with a wooden spoon, until the butter and sugar have both melted.

4 Remove the pan from the heat and pour the melted mixture over the bananas.

5 Put the dish under the grill [broiler] and grill [broil] for 5 to 8 minutes or until the mixture is bubbly.

6 Remove the dish from the grill [broiler] and serve it at once, or allow to cool before serving.

Creamy Orange Snow tart

This is a super tart made with a crunchy biscuit [cookie] crust instead of pastry. It has the most gorgeous filling and doesn't need to be baked. If you like, you can decorate the top with chocolate drops or flaked chocolate.

You Will Need
for a 20.5 cm [8-inch] tart

75 g [⅜ cup] butter

150 g crushed digestive biscuits [1½ cups crushed graham crackers]. To crush the biscuits [crackers] put them between two sheets of greaseproof or waxed paper on the table and, with a rolling pin, roll backwards and forwards until they are finely crushed. Don't leave any lumps!

2 eggs

100 g [½ cup] castor sugar

1 orange

2 teaspoons gelatine

4 tablespoons hot water

142 ml double cream [⅝ cup heavy cream]

1 In a small saucepan, melt the butter over low heat. (Don't let the butter get brown or it will taste burnt.) Remove the pan from the heat and stir in the crushed biscuits [cookies].

2 Place a loose-bottomed cake tin (about 20.5 cm [8-inches] across) on the table.

6 Grate the orange rind finely. Then cut the orange in half and squeeze all the juice into a bowl, set aside.

7 In a small bowl, mix the gelatine with the hot water until it has completely dissolved. Set it aside.

9 Wash and dry the whisk well. In a medium-sized mixing bowl, beat the egg whites with a wire whisk or rotary beater until they are stiff. (For how to do this, see page 5.)

10 With a metal spoon, gently mix in the remaining sugar. Then, using the wire whisk or rotary beater, whisk the egg white mixture into the orange mixture.

30

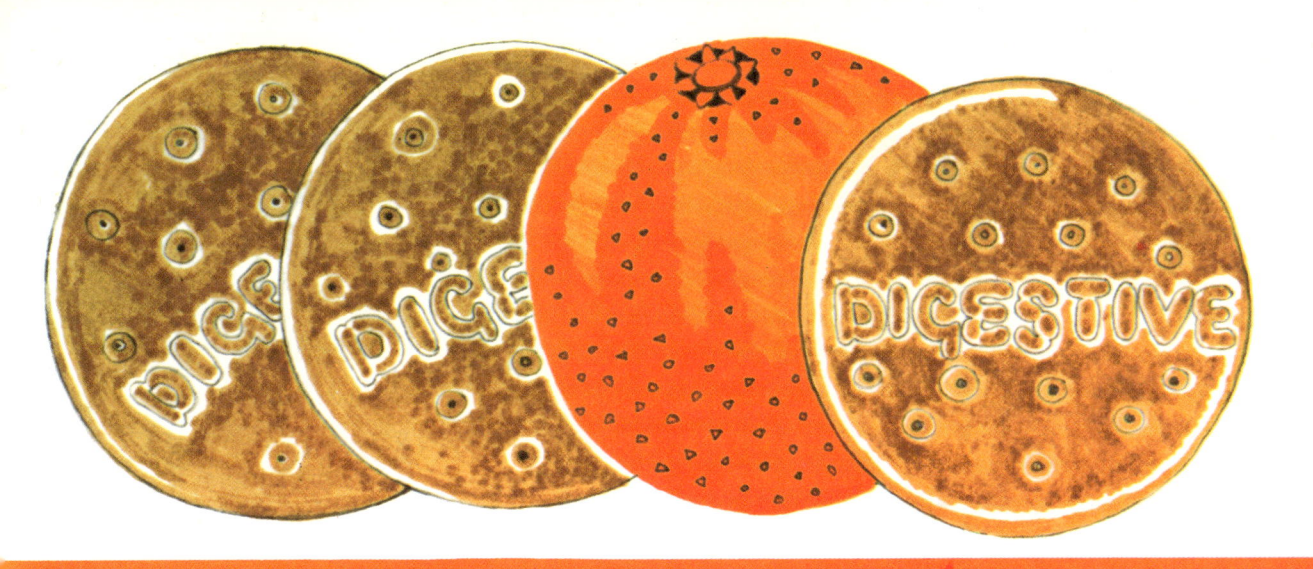

3 Press the crumb mixture firmly on to the bottom and around the sides of the cake tin. Place the tin in the refrigerator to chill for 30 minutes or until the crumb crust has set.

4 Separate the eggs (for how to do this, see page 5). Set the egg whites aside. Put the yolks and half of the sugar in a heatproof bowl. Put the bowl over a pan half-filled with hot water.

5 Put the pan on low heat and, using a wire whisk, whisk until the mixture is creamy and begins to thicken. Remove the pan from the heat and set aside to cool.

8 Stir the orange rind and juice into the cooled egg yolk mixture, then stir in the gelatine. Keep stirring until the mixture is well mixed. Set it aside.

12 Remove the tart from the refrigerator. Press up on the loose bottom of the tin and, with the help of a knife, slide the tart on to a serving plate.

11 Stir in the cream, then spoon the mixture into the crumb crust. Return the cake tin to the refrigerator and chill for 2 hours or until the filling is set.

31

Meat Pasties

You Will Need
for 8 pasties

- 300 g [3 cups] frozen shortcrust pastry dough (don't forget to thaw it out before you use it, though!)
- 2 onions
- 1 slice streaky bacon
- 1 tablespoon flour
- 4 tablespoons cold water or stock
- ¼ teaspoon salt
- ¼ teaspoon pepper
- ¼ teaspoon dried marjoram (optional)
- ¼ teaspoon paprika (optional)
- 150 g [6 oz] corned beef, chopped up into small pieces

Before you begin, turn on the oven to fairly hot 400°F (Gas Mark 6, 200°C).

Pasties can be filled with almost anything that takes your fancy and this recipe has a particularly delicious filling mixture—beef and onion. Take some Meat Pasties with you on your next picnic! You will need a mincer [grinder] or food mill for this recipe.

32

1 On a pastry board which has been sprinkled with a little flour, roll out the dough to about 6 cm [¼-inch] thick.

2 Use a pastry cutter or a small cup or glass to press out circles of dough. You will need 8 circles about 7.5 cm [3-inches] across and 8 circles about 6 cm [2½-inches] across.

3 Press the larger circles into a tin of patty-pans. (Or you can use separate little aluminium foil pans.) Set them aside while you make the filling.

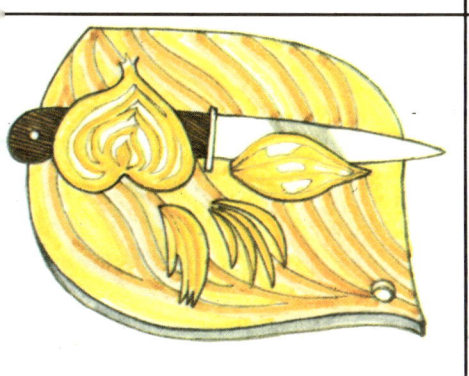

4 Cut off the ends from the onions and peel off their outer skin. Place the onions on a chopping board and with a knife, cut them into slices.

5 Put the slice of bacon and the onions through a mincer [grinder] or food mill.

6 Put the minced [ground] mixture into a frying-pan and cook it over low heat, stirring occasionally, until the onions are soft but not brown. Watch carefully while it's cooking—if it becomes too dry, add a little butter.

7 When the onions are soft, stir in the flour and cook, stirring constantly, for 1 minute.

8 Stir in the cold water or stock, the salt, pepper, marjoram and paprika (if you are using them). Heat the mixture until the water boils, then stir in the corned beef.

9 Remove the pan from the heat. Put a heaped tablespoonful of the meat mixture into each lined patty-pan.

10 Put on the lids of the pasties (the smaller dough circles), pressing the edges down firmly with your fingers to seal in the filling.

11 With a knife, make a little hole in the centre of each pasty so that the steam can escape while the pasty is cooking.

12 Put the pasties into the oven and bake them for 20 minutes. If the pastry is not light brown at this point, bake for a few minutes longer. Then remove from the oven and cool.

Bread

This delicious and nutritious home-made bread has a slightly rough, mealie texture which makes it particularly delicious served slightly warm with lots of butter and thick slices of cheese.

You Will Need
for one medium-sized loaf

½ teaspoon butter

12½ g [½ oz] dried yeast

1 teaspoon sugar

1 tablespoon lukewarm water

300 g plain flour [3 cups all-purpose flour]

100 g wholemeal flour [1 cup wholewheat flour]

1 teaspoon salt

284 ml [1¼ cups] lukewarm water

2 tablespoons wheat germ

1 With the ½ teaspoon of butter, lightly grease a 20 cm by 10 cm [8-inch by 4-inch] loaf tin and set it aside.

2 Put the yeast, sugar and the tablespoon of water into a bowl. With a fork, beat until they form a smooth paste. Set in a warm place for 20 minutes or until the yeast is frothy.

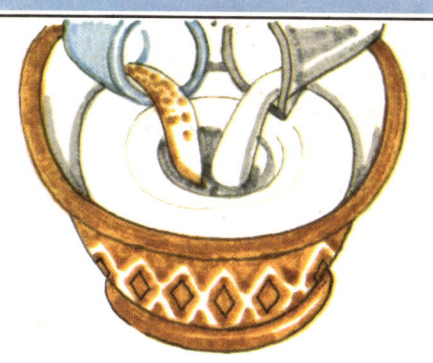

3 Put the flour, wholemeal [wholewheat] flour and salt into a large, mixing bowl. Make a hollow in the centre and pour in the yeast and the 284 ml [1¼ cups] of lukewarm water.

4 Using your fingers, gradually draw the flour into the liquid. Continue mixing until all the flour is incorporated and the dough comes away from the sides of the bowl.

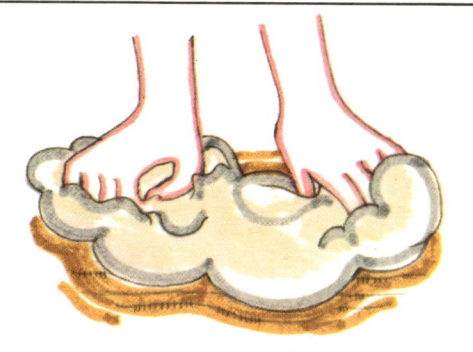

5 Turn the dough out on to a lightly floured board or marble slab and knead it for about 10 minutes. (For how to do this see page 5.)

6 Shape the dough into a loaf and put it into the tin. Cover with a damp cloth and set aside in the warm place for 1½ hours or until the dough has risen to the top of the tin.

7 Ten minutes before the rising time is up, turn on the oven to very hot 475°F (Gas Mark 9, 240°C).

8 At the end of the rising time, uncover the tin and sprinkle the wheat germ over the top of the loaf.

9 Place the tin in the centre of the oven and bake the bread for 15 minutes.

10 Reduce the temperature to hot 425°F (Gas Mark 7, 220°C) and bake for 30 minutes. The bread should be golden. If it is not, bake for a few minutes longer. Remove from the oven.

11 To test whether the bread is cooked tip the loaf out of the tin and rap the underside with your knuckles. If the bread sounds hollow, like a drum, it is cooked.

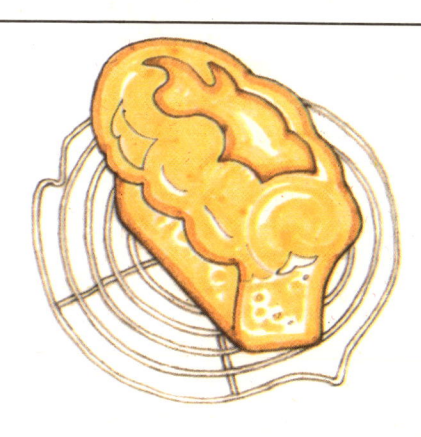

12 When the bread is cooked, put it on a wire rack to cool before serving.

Queen of Puddings

You Will Need
for 4 people

1 teaspoon butter
4 slices stale white bread
25 g [3 tablespoons] custard powder
2 tablespoons sugar
568 ml [2½ cups] milk
2 egg whites
4 tablespoons castor sugar
4 tablespoons jam (use a good chunky one like strawberry or apricot for the best results)

Next time you want to give your mother a treat, why not make her this splendid hot pudding? It's crowned with a delicious meringue topping.

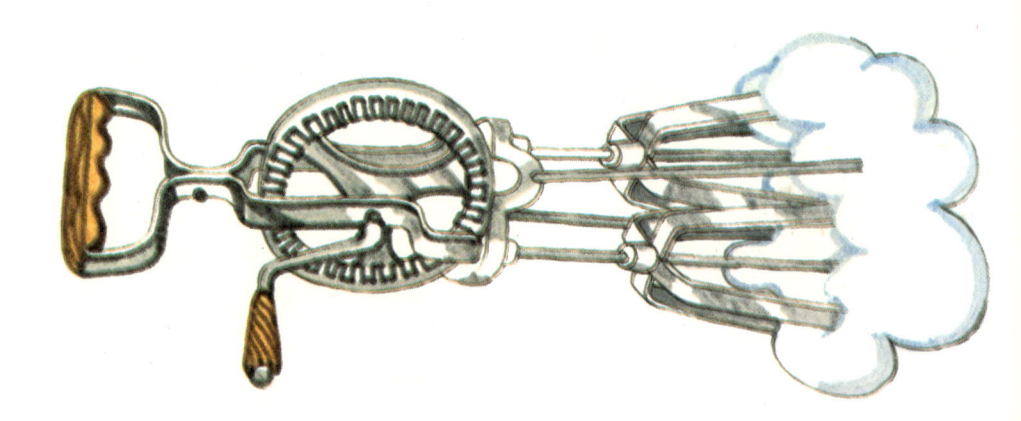

1 With the teaspoon of butter grease a medium-sized ovenproof pie dish. Set aside.

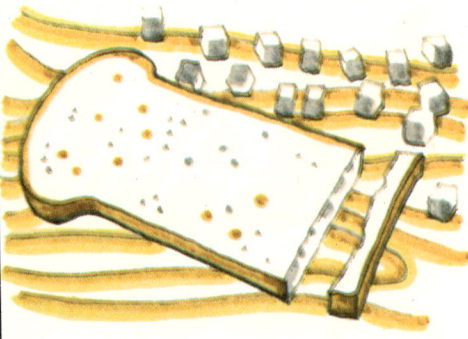

2 Cut off the crusts from the bread and throw them away. Then cut the bread into small cubes and put it into the pie dish.

3 In a large bowl, mix the custard powder and the 2 tablespoons of sugar together. Stir in 3 tablespoons of the milk and beat well until the ingredients form a smooth paste.

4 Pour the rest of the milk into a saucepan and put the pan over low heat. Heat the milk until it is hot. (Keep watching the milk while it heats—don't let it boil over.)

5 When the milk is just beginning to bubble, quickly remove the pan from the heat. Pour the milk on to the custard mixture, stirring constantly to prevent any lumps from forming.

6 Pour the mixture back into the pan again and return the pan to low heat. Cook, stirring with a wooden spoon for 2 minutes or until the custard boils

7 Remove the pan from the heat and pour the custard over the bread cubes in the pie dish. Set the dish aside for 15 minutes to allow the custard to soak into the bread.

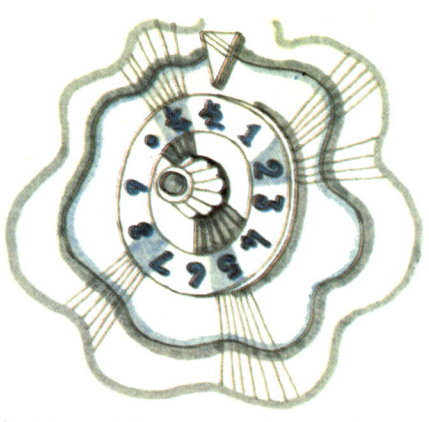

8 Meanwhile, turn on the oven to very cool 250°F (Gas Mark ½, 130°C).

9 Now make the meringue topping. In a medium-sized bowl, beat the egg whites with a wire whisk or rotary beater until they are stiff. (For how to do this see page 5.)

10 When the whites are quite stiff, sprinkle over 2 tablespoons of the castor sugar and continue whisking until they are very stiff.

11 Sprinkle on the remaining castor sugar, and, using a metal spoon, gently fold it in.

12 Spread the jam over the custard then the egg whites. Put the dish in the oven and bake for 30 minutes. If the meringue is pale gold it is cooked and should be served immediately.

37

Shortbread

You Will Need
for about 16 biscuits [cookies]

- 150 g [1½ cups] flour
- ¼ teaspoon salt
- 100 g [½ cup] butter, cut into small pieces
- 50 g [¼ cup] castor sugar
- 1 teaspoon butter
- 1 tablespoon flour

Before you begin, turn on the oven to warm 325°F (Gas Mark 3, 170°C).

The Scots are generally thought to have 'invented' shortbread and a marvellous invention it is. Serve these melt-in-the-mouth biscuits [cookies] with mugs of hot chocolate and just watch them disappear!

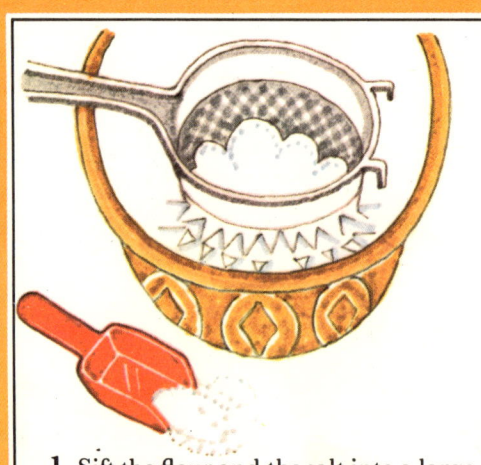

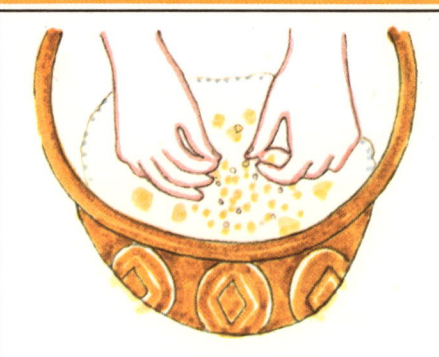

1 Sift the flour and the salt into a large mixing bowl.

2 Using your fingertips, rub the butter pieces gently into the flour until the mixture is very crumbly and has no large lumps.

3 Mix in the castor sugar and, using your hands, squeeze the mixture together until it forms a large ball.

4 On a pastry board that has been lightly sprinkled with flour, roll out the dough to about 1.3 cm [½-inch] thick. Make the edges neat with a knife so that the dough forms a rectangle.

5 Using a knife, lightly mark the dough into 7.5 cm [3-inch] by 3.8 cm [1½-inch] bars. (Don't cut through the dough—it should be baked in one piece.)

6 With any leftover bits, you could make some small biscuits [cookies] shaping them into fancy shapes with pastry cutters—try hearts, or diamonds or circles.

7 Using the teaspoon of butter, lightly grease a medium-sized baking sheet. Sprinkle the sheet with the tablespoon of flour, shaking the tray to distribute the flour evenly all over.

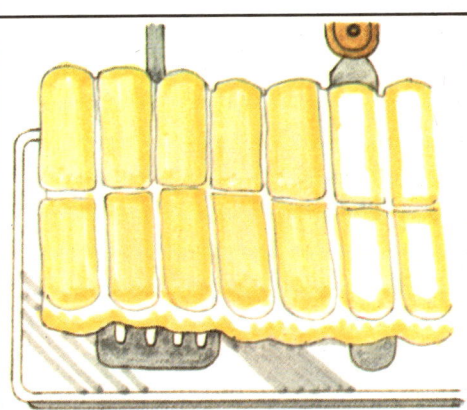

8 Carefully lift the dough on to the baking sheet (you may find a fish slice or spatula is useful for this).

9 With a fork, prick holes all over the top of the dough (this will help the dough bake evenly).

10 Put the sheet in the oven and bake the shortbread for 45 minutes to 1 hour. When the shortbread is golden brown and firm it is cooked and should be removed from the oven.

11 Let the shortbread cool on the baking sheet for 10 minutes.

12 Cut the shortbread into bars and transfer the bars to a wire rack to cool completely. Sprinkle the bars with a little castor sugar, for an extra-special professional touch.

Liver, Bacon and Apple Hot Pot

You Will Need
for 4 people

- 600 g [1½ lb] cooking apples
- 2 medium-sized onions
- 284 ml [1¼ cups] boiling water
- 1 beef stock cube
- 600 g [1½ lb] lamb's liver (ask the butcher to cut it into six ¼-inch slices)
- ⅛ teaspoon salt
- ½ teaspoon black pepper
- 350 g [14 oz] canned peeled tomatoes
- 4 lean bacon slices

Before you begin, turn on the oven to moderate 350°F (Gas Mark 4, 180°C).

This is a perfect Sunday lunch or supper dish. Make it for your family and give your mother a Sunday holiday from the kitchen. If you're feeling really hungry, serve Liver, Bacon and Apple Hot Pot with mashed potatoes and peas, with Strawberry Trifle for dessert.

1 Using a knife, peel, core and slice the apples.

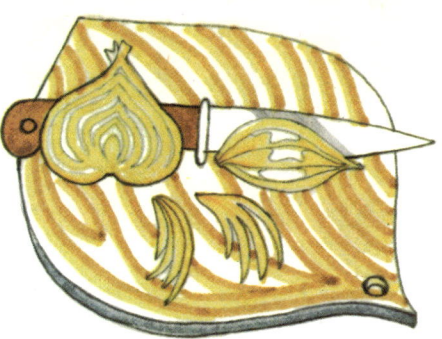

2 Cut off the ends from the onion and peel off its outer skin. Place the onion on a chopping board and cut it into thin slices. Set the apple and onion slices aside.

3 Pour the boiling water into a large jug and add the stock cube. Stir briskly with a fork or spoon until the cube has completely dissolved. Set aside.

4 Spread half of the apple and onion slices over the bottom of an ovenproof casserole.

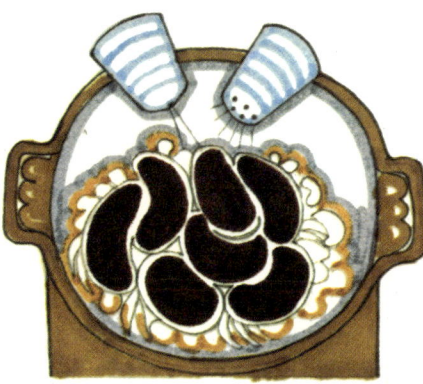

5 Lay the liver slices in a layer on top of the apples and onions, then sprinkle over the salt and pepper.

6 Drain the tomatoes through a strainer held over a bowl. (Keep the juice—it's good to drink.) Place the tomatoes on top of the liver.

7 Then arrange the remaining apple and onion slices on top of the tomatoes.

8 Pour the beef stock into the casserole.

9 Finally, carefully lay the bacon slices on top of the mixture.

10 Put the lid on the casserole or cover it with aluminium foil.

11 Place the casserole in the oven and bake the liver mixture for 1½ hours.

12 Wearing oven gloves, remove the hot pot from the oven and serve it straight from the casserole.

41

Chocolate Fudge

Fudge is fun to make and absolutely scrumptious to eat— you'll want to eat more than one or two pieces of this delicious Chocolate Fudge—so make lots!

You Will Need
for about 45 sweets [candies]

1 teaspoon butter

50 g dark [2 squares semi-sweet] cooking chocolate

400 g [2 cups] sugar

142 ml [5/8 cup] milk

50 g [1/4 cup] butter

1 With the teaspoon of butter, lightly grease a 20.5 cm [8-inch] square cake tin. Set it aside.

2 Break up the chocolate into small pieces. (Try not to eat any—this fudge is best when it is *really* chocolatey.)

3 Put the chocolate pieces, the sugar and milk into a medium-sized heavy saucepan.

4 Put the saucepan over moderate heat and cook the mixture, stirring constantly with a wooden spoon, until the chocolate has melted and the sugar has dissolved.

5 Increase the heat to high. Ask your mother to do this for you, especially if you have a gas stove.

6 Bring the mixture to the boil. (If it starts to rise to the rim of the pan, remove it from the heat.) Reduce the heat to moderate again and boil for 5 minutes, stirring occasionally.

7 The mixture should be thick enough now. To test to see whether it is, put a little on the wooden spoon and dip it into a bowl of cold water—the mixture should form a soft ball.

8 When the fudge is thick enough, remove the pan from the heat and set it aside for 5 minutes so that the mixture can cool a bit.

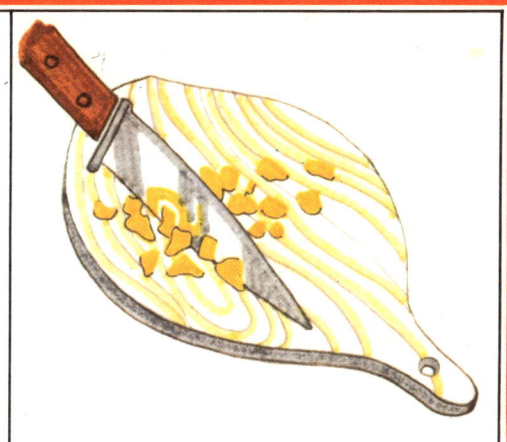

9 Cut the butter into small pieces with a knife.

10 Add the butter a piece at a time and stir with the spoon. Keep stirring until all the butter has been added and has melted into the mixture. (The mixture should be smooth.)

11 Pour the fudge mixture into the prepared cake tin and set it aside for 10 minutes.

12 Then, with a knife, mark the fudge into squares. Set it aside to harden completely before breaking it up into squares and serving.

43

Fairy Cakes

Light as gossamer, that's what fairy cakes are AND they're marvellous to eat—so serve them at your next party or when you next have a friend to tea!

You Will Need
for 16-18 cakes

16-18 pretty paper cake cases

50 g [⅓ cup] sultanas or seedless raisins or chopped glacé cherries

1 tablespoon flour

100 g [½ cup] soft butter

100 g [½ cup] castor sugar

2 eggs

1 teaspoon vanilla essence

100 g [1 cup] self-raising flour

8-9 glacé cherries, halved (for decoration)

For icing

150 g icing sugar [1½ cups confectioners' sugar]

¼ teaspoon lemon flavouring

3 tablespoons warm water

3 drops yellow food colouring

Before you begin, turn on the oven to moderate 350°F (Gas Mark 4, 180°C).

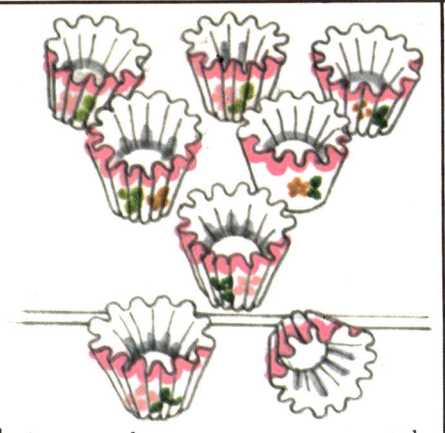

1 Arrange the paper cases on a metal baking sheet.

2 Wash, drain and dry the sultanas or raisins. (If you're using glacé cherries, you don't need to wash them.)

3 Put the sultanas or raisins or cherries in a bowl, then sprinkle the tablespoon of flour over the top. Shake the bowl gently to coat the fruit with the flour.

4 Put the butter and sugar into a large bowl, and using a wooden spoon beat them together. When they are well creamed add the eggs and beat them in.

5 Now sift in the self-raising flour and lightly fold it in. When the mixture is smooth, mix in the sultanas or raisins or chopped cherries and mix well.

6 Put about 1 heaped tablespoonful of the mixture into each paper case—use a metal spoon for this. And when you're finished, the bowl will be well worth licking!

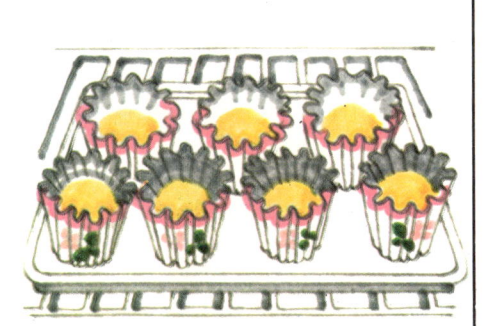

7 Put the filled paper cases on the baking sheet into the oven and bake the cakes for 15 minutes.

8 When they are golden on top and firm to touch they are cooked and can be removed from the oven. Set them aside to cool.

9 To make the icing, sift the icing [confectioners'] sugar into a medium-sized bowl. (This is sifted so there won't be any lumps.)

10 Add the lemon flavouring and stir to mix. Add the warm water, a drop at a time, stirring until the icing is very smooth. Mix in the yellow food colouring.

11 To ice the cakes, drop enough icing on to each cake to cover the top. Spread evenly over the tops with the blade of a knife.

12 Put half a glacé cherry on top of each cake and set the cakes aside until the icing sets.

45

Mince Pies

It doesn't have to be Christmas to make Mince Pies. They're so delicious—hot or cold—especially when they're served with cream, custard or ice-cream. You can buy commercially-prepared mincemeat in jars at most supermarkets.

You Will Need
for about 12 pies

300 g [3 cups] frozen shortcrust dough (don't forget to thaw it out before you use it!)

300 g [12 oz] mincemeat

1 egg

1 tablespoon castor sugar

Special Topping

1 egg white

142 ml double cream [$\frac{5}{8}$ cup heavy cream]

Before you begin, turn on the oven to fairly hot 400°F (Gas Mark 6, 200°C).

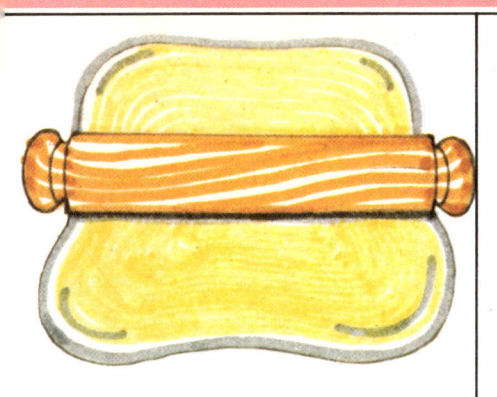

1 On a pastry board that has been sprinkled with a little flour, roll out the dough to about .6 cm [¼-inch] thick.

2 Use a pastry cutter or a small cup or glass to press out circles of dough. You will need 12 circles about 6 cm [2½-inches] across and 12 about 5 cm [2-inches] across.

3 Press the larger circles into a tin of patty-pans. (Or you can use separate little aluminium foil pans.)

4 Put a heaped tablespoonful of mincemeat into each patty-pan.

5 Break the egg into a cup (for how to do this, see page 5). Beat the egg thoroughly with a fork.

6 With a pastry brush, or a clean finger, brush a little of the beaten egg along all the edges of the dough.

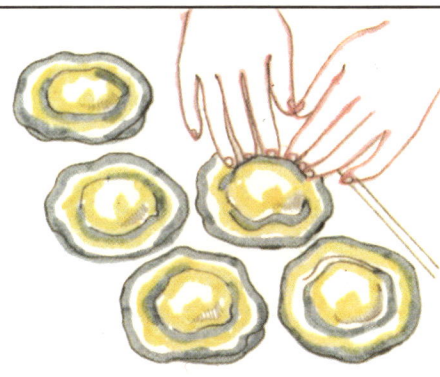

7 Put on the lids of the pies (the smaller dough circles) pressing the edges down firmly with your fingers to seal in the filling.

8 With a knife, make a little hole in the centre of each pie so that the steam can escape while the pies are baking.

9 Put the patty-pans into the oven and bake the pies for 20 minutes. If the pastry is not light brown and crisp at this stage, bake for a few minutes longer. Then remove from the oven.

10 Let the pies cool a little in the patty-pans. Then carefully take them out of the pans and sprinkle a little castor sugar over the tops before you serve them.

11 Here's a special topping for the pies. In a medium-sized bowl beat the egg white with a wire whisk or rotary beater until it forms a peak. (For how to do this, see page 5.)

12 In another bowl, whisk the double [heavy] cream until it becomes thick. Then, using a metal spoon, mix the egg white into it. Spoon the mixture over the pies and—mmm . . .

Toad in the Hole

You Will Need
for 4 people

Toad in the Hole is as English as Big Ben. Serve it for supper with baked beans.

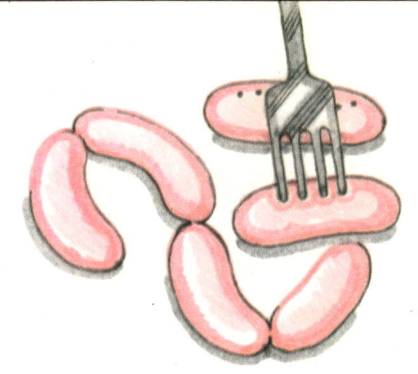

400 g [1 lb] sausages
100 g [1 cup] flour
⅛ teaspoon salt
¼ teaspoon white pepper
1 egg
284 ml [1¼ cups] milk

Before you begin, turn on the oven to hot 425°F (Gas Mark 7, 220°C).

1 Separate the sausages, and, using a fork, prick their skins once or twice. (This is so they won't burst during cooking.)

2 Put all of the sausages on the bottom of a large ovenproof dish. Then put the dish into the oven and bake the sausages for 10 minutes.

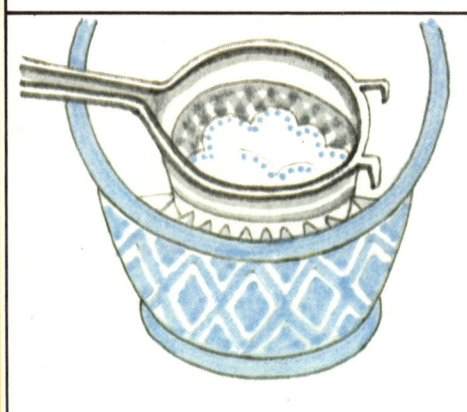

3 While the sausages are baking, sift the flour, salt and pepper into a large bowl.

4 Make a well in the centre of the flour and add the egg and half of the milk. Mix well, then pour in the rest of the milk and beat well until the batter is very smooth.

5 Take the baking dish out of the oven and pour the batter over the sausages.

6 Return the dish to the oven and bake for 35 minutes. If the top is not brown at this stage, bake for a few minutes longer. Then remove from the oven and serve immediately!

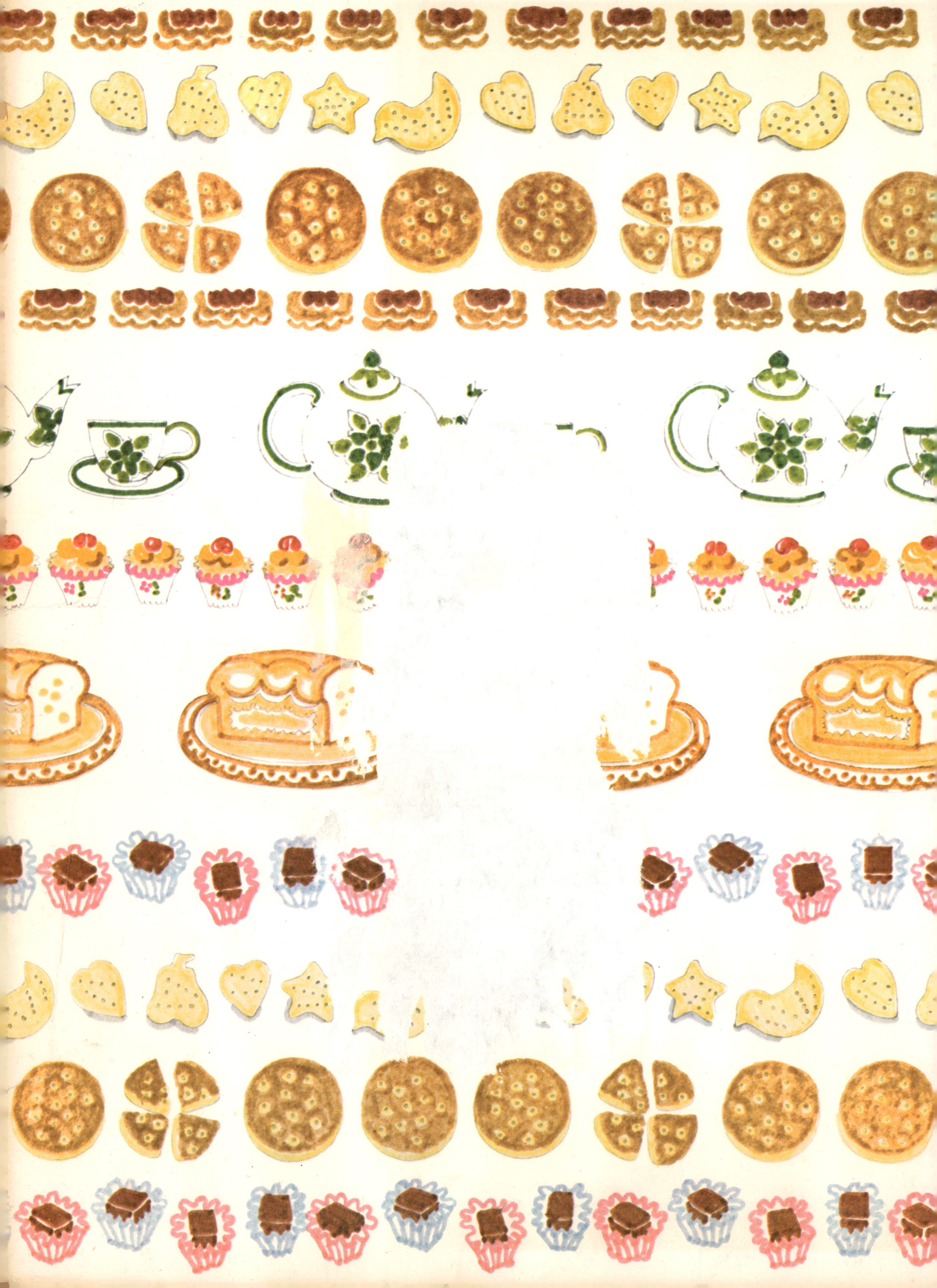